Test Your English Vocabulary in Use

Upper-intermediate

Michael McCarthy
Felicity O'Dell

CAMBRIDGE
UNIVERSITY PRESS

CAMBRIDGE UNIVERSITY PRESS
Cambridge, New York, Melbourne, Madrid, Cape Town, Singapore,
São Paulo, Delhi, Dubai, Tokyo

Cambridge University Press
The Edinburgh Building, Cambridge CB2 8RU, UK

www.cambridge.org
Information on this title: www.cambridge.org/9780521665681

First published 2001
9th printing 2010

Printed in the United Kingdom at the University Press, Cambridge

A catalogue record for this publication is available from the British Library

ISBN 978-0-521-66568-1 Edition with answers

Contents

Topics

Feelings and actions

Basic concepts

Acknowledgements

We are very grateful to all the schools, institutions, teachers and students around the world who either piloted or commented on the material.

Matylda Arabas, Gydnia, Poland
Tim Bromley, Bath, UK
Melanie Chrisp, Hove, UK
Celso Frade, São Paulo, Brazil
Sue Derry Penz, Cambridge, UK
Susi Dobler, London, UK
Ludmila Gorodetskaya, Moscow, Russia
Marie Homerová, Prague, Czech Republic
Thomas Hull, Rennes, France
Tatyana Kazarritskaya, Moscow, Russia
Zdena Křížová, Prague, Czech Republic
Ewa Gumul, Sosnowiec, Poland
Sally McLaren, Fondi, Italy
Magdolna Lutring, Budapest, Hungary
Geraldine Mark, Cheltenham, UK
Barbara Murphy, Seoul, South Korea
Ewa Modrzejewska, Gdańsk, Poland
Nobuhiro Nakamura, Fukushima-ken, Japan
Hee-suk Park, Namseoul University, Korea
Andrea Paul, Melbourne, Australia
M Ramzy Radwan, Cairo, Egypt
Davee Schulte, Seoul, South Korea
Margaret Squibb, Trento, Italy
Susan Tesar, Cambridge, UK
Michael Valpy, Hove, UK
Giles Witton Davies, Taipei, Taiwan
Tadeusz Z. Wolański, Gdańsk, Poland
Inas Mohammed Younis, Cairo, Egypt

We would also like to thank our editors at Cambridge University Press, in particular Nóirín Burke and Geraldine Mark, whose expertise has enabled us to produce a much better book than we could have done alone.

Introduction to the student

Why test vocabulary?

Research has shown that you need to meet a word at least 7 times before you know it properly. Doing exercises like these, that practise words and expressions that you have already encountered, is a useful way of helping yourself to fix the vocabulary you are working on in your long-term memory.

What vocabulary is tested?

This book provides a series of tests on different aspects of English vocabulary at an upper-intermediate level. It is based on the vocabulary presented and practised in the units of *English Vocabulary in Use: upper-intermediate*. There are references in the contents pages and in each test to show you which unit or units each test is based on. In a few cases vocabulary items are included which have not been presented in *English Vocabulary in Use* and, when this happens, the instructions for the exercise suggest that you may use a dictionary if you wish. You can, of course, use these tests even if you have not been working with *English Vocabulary in Use* but are simply interested in assessing your knowledge of the vocabulary area covered by the test.

How do I score my tests?

Each test is scored out of 40 and a key, with information about how many marks each item gets, is given at the back of the book. It should be very clear from the key what you need to write to get each mark and so you should be able to score your work without a teacher, if you wish to. The first exercise in each test always offers a maximum score of 10 and it is recommended that you do this exercise first. If your score for this exercise is less than 5, then we suggest that you do a bit more work in the language area covered by the test before doing the rest of it.

Although the tests are all scored out of 40, you will probably feel that some tests are easier than others. This is partly because everyone is more familiar with some vocabulary areas than others. However, because certain vocabulary areas are particularly dense, it is also true that in a few cases you need to show that you know more words and expressions than you do to get the same number of marks in the rest of the tests.

How long do the tests take?

Each test should take 20 to 30 minutes to complete.

We hope that you enjoy using these tests and that they will help you to learn the vocabulary that you want and need to master at this level.

1 Names of English language words

1.1

10 marks

Find each of the following in the text below.

Example: a singular noun **book**

1 an article
2 an adjective
3 one plural noun
4 a preposition
5 an adverb

6 an uncountable noun
7 an irregular verb
8 an example of a phrase
9 an example of a sentence
10 an example of a collocation

> The aim of this book is to help you test your knowledge of English vocabulary. Think about the questions carefully and then check your answers in the back of the book.

1.2

5 marks

Draw the following punctuation marks.

1 full stop ....
2 apostrophe ....
3 question mark ....

4 hyphen ....
5 colon ....

1.3

5 marks

Name these punctuation marks.

1 ( ) ....
2 , ...
3 ! ....

4 ; ....
5 " " ....

1.4

20 marks

Answer these questions.

1 What are the prefix, the root and the suffix in *disorganisation*?
2 How many syllables are there in the word *monosyllabic*, and which one is stressed?
3 Name a noun, a verb, an adjective and an adverb based on the root *wide*.
4 Give a synonym and an antonym for *wide*.
5 Give a colloquial synonym for *man*.
6 What is the main verb in the sentence below? What are its subject and its object?

> English has a very large vocabulary, which adds greatly to our opportunities to express subtle shades of meaning and to use different styles.

7 In the sentence above, is the verb *adds* used transitively or intransitively? What about *express*?
8 *Pig-headed* and *determined* can be synonyms. Which of these words is pejorative?
9 Who would we normally speak to using informal English?
10 What is a collocation?

Your score

/40

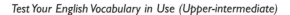

TEST

2 Suffixes

2.1
10 marks

Put *-er* or *-or* onto the endings of these words, as appropriate.

Example: read.**er**...

1 paint........
2 doct........
3 act........
4 sail........
5 writ........

6 work........
7 supervis........
8 project........
9 print........
10 pencil-sharpen........

2.2
10 marks

Make nouns from these verbs using *-tion, -ion* or *-ssion.*

Example: permit: permission

1 pollute
2 impress
3 alter
4 admit
5 complicate

6 reduce
7 add
8 donate
9 explain
10 promote

2.3
10 marks

What do we call ...?

1 A person who plays the piano?
2 A person who believes in the ideas of Karl Marx?
3 The person to whom a letter is addressed?
4 A person who types letters and other documents?
5 A person who is employed by someone?

2.4
5 marks

Add the *-ness* suffix to these adjectives.

Example: tired: tiredness

1 sad
2 happy
3 crazy
4 hopeless
5 ready

2.5
5 marks

Circle the correct suffixed form of these words.

Example: **beautiful**   beautyise   (beautify)   beauticate

1 **refuse**   refusation   refusal   refusity
2 **forget**   forgetful   forgetty   forgetish
3 **commercial**   commercify   commerciate   commercialise
4 **excite**   excital   exciteship   excitement
5 **scarce**   scarcity   scarcedom   scarcement

Your score

/40

TEST

3 Prefixes

3.1
10 marks

Read horizontally or vertically (not diagonally) to find the meanings of these prefixes in the word-square.

Example: bi as in bicycle

1 multi as in multi-national
2 pre as in pre-war
3 anti as in antisocial
4 pseudo as in pseudo-scientific
5 semi as in semi-circle
6 micro as in microscopic
7 mono as in monologue
8 mis as in misunderstand
9 re as in re-read
10 sub as in submarine

W	L	I	R	W	T	A	S
B	I	A	D	R	O	D	O
I	N	G	R	O	N	E	B
A	G	A	I	N	S	T	E
N	H	I	A	G	M	O	F
M	A	N	Y	L	A	E	O
T	L	A	D	Y	L	S	R
W	F	O	F	A	L	S	E
O	U	N	D	E	R	O	N

3.2
10 marks

Add a prefix to a word in the first statement in order to make an opposite word that completes the responses.

Example: That man's locking the door.   No he isn't. He's ~~unlocking~~ it.

1 He's quite mature for his age.   I don't agree. I think he's ....
2 I think she's reliable.   No she isn't. She's very ....
3 Is she wrapping that parcel?   No, she's .... it.
4 Is his handwriting legible?   No, I find it quite ....
5 Does her father approve of Jack?   No, he .... of him.
6 Do you think he's honest?   No, I'm sure he's ....
7 Is it convenient to have a chat?   No, sorry, it's a bit .... now.
8 Can I replace the vase I broke?   I'm afraid not – it's ....
9 Do you like your boss?   No, I .... him intensely.
10 Are these mushrooms edible?   No, I'm pretty sure they're ....

3.3
10 marks

Use your knowledge of prefixes to write definitions of the underlined words.

Although Jim is an (1)ex-soldier, he's only (2)semi-literate. When he tries to write a letter, he (3)misspells half the words and his wife has to (4)rewrite it for him. His wife used to work in a (5)sub-department of the post office where her main job was (6)redirecting mail. Jim's very (7)pro-army but he (8)over-emphasises its good points. His wife, on the other hand, is rather (9)anti-army and she (10)undervalues its positive aspects.

3.4
10 marks

Which word is the odd one out in each set?

Example: legible, loyal, legal, legitimate   *loyal – it forms its opposite with dis–*
                whereas the others use the prefix il–

1 insert, internal, inedible, income
2 disobey, disconnect, dismount, dissimilar
3 uncomfortable, unlock, unfold, unzip
4 extract, ex-wife, ex-communicate, exhale
5 reversible, rational, reasonable, relevant

Your score
/40

4 Roots

4.1

10 marks

Choose one of the words from the box. Put it in the correct form to complete the sentences. Note that the words in the box are all verbs. Sometimes you have to change the verb into a noun, adjective or adverb.

advertise	divert	~~express~~	introduce	postpone	support

Example: Why do you have such a strange _expression_ on your face?

1 The meeting .... until 4 p.m.
2 If you are looking for a temporary job, read the .... in the local paper.
3 Our neighbours behaved very .... when my mother was ill.
4 Charlie's arrival created a .... and I managed to leave without being noticed.
5 The shop has a very good .... offer on a new brand of biscuits.

4.2

16 marks

Complete the box. Use a dictionary if necessary.

verb	person noun	adjective	abstract noun
	oppressor		oppression
prospect			
produce			
	composer		
		deported	
convert	convert		

4.3

5 marks

Match the Latin roots on the left with their meanings on the right.

1 duc, duct   a carry, take
2 port   b turn
3 pose, pone   c look, see
4 press   d place, put
5 spect   e lead
6 vert   f press, push

4.4

9 marks

Find words from one of the roots in 4.3 to fit the definitions.

Example: to look up to, admire   _respect_

1 products brought into a country from another country   ....
2 a person the police think may have committed a crime   ....
3 a person who leads an orchestra   ....
4 inward-looking   ....
5 to persuade someone to change their beliefs   ....
6 the first part of an essay or thesis   ....
7 making you feel miserable   ....
8 a person who checks that things are done correctly   ....
9 to put someone off their throne   ....

TEST

5 Abstract nouns

5.1

10 marks

Make abstract nouns from the words in the box below. Put them in the correct column.

~~absurd~~	achieve	adult	combine	complex	deep	excite	free
friend	friendly	generous	imagine	member	mother	owner
prosperous	recognise	tender	ugly	wide	wise

-ment	-ion	-ness	-ship	-ity	-dom	-hood	-th
				absurdity			

5.2

10 marks

Complete the sentences by forming an abstract noun from the word in brackets at the end of the sentence.

Example: His face was so red with ..._anger_.......... that I thought he would have a heart attack there and then. (angry)

1 The cat purred with .... as it drank the cream. (satisfy)
2 Rose has a rather difficult .... with her father. (relate)
3 His writing shows a great deal of .... (sensitive)
4 Sal hasn't ever known true .... with Bill. (happy)
5 Dick hasn't much of a sense of .... (humorous)
6 Patrick is looking forward to his .... (retire)
7 Penny always showed great .... to me. (kind)
8 I wonder if women will ever achieve full .... (equal)
9 I don't think I've ever experienced .... (bored)
10 This work is spoiled by the student's .... (care)

5.3

10 marks

Put these abstract nouns into the correct column: pleasant or unpleasant.

| discouragement | improvement | hostility | rage | brotherhood |
| companionship | faith | bitterness | luck | calm | fear |

pleasant	unpleasant
	discouragement

5.4

10 marks

Add two extra abstract nouns to each of the columns in 5.1. Write down 4 other abstract nouns which do not use a suffix, e.g. love. Do not write down any of the words already on this page.

Your score

/40

6 Compound adjectives

6.1 Fill in the other part of these compound adjectives. Choose from the words in the box.

10 marks

controlled	~~fetched~~	free	haired	minded
new	pink	proof	top	up	world

Example: a far-..*fetched*.... excuse

1 a shocking-..................... blouse
2 a remote-..................... toy
3 ....-secret information
4 an absent-..................... professor
5 a sugar-..................... diet

6 brand-..................... clothes
7 a ....-famous star
8 hard-..................... students
9 a bullet-..................... car
10 curly-..................... baby

6.2 Find different ways of completing these compounds. Use words from the box.

10 marks

blonde	blue	class	dark	hand	~~interest~~
rate	round	short	straight	~~sugar~~	tax

Examples: sugar   2 ....   3 ....   4 ....
            interest-free   ....-haired   ....-eyed   first-.....................
         1 ....

6.3 Match the adjectives in box A with the nouns they are often used with in box B.

10 marks *Example:* hard-working students

A
air-conditioned	long-distance
time-consuming	off-peak
open-necked	built-up
all-out	well-off
cut-price	~~hard working~~
far-fetched	

B
ideas	rooms
areas	work
middle classes	strike
runner	phone calls
goods	shirt
~~students~~	

6.4 Put the words in order to make common compound adjective + noun collocations. Then explain the meaning of the compound adjective.

10 marks

Example: laugh / hearted / light   light-hearted laugh: light-hearted = carefree

1 headed / big / man
2 coat / worn / out
3 never / lecture / ending
4 witted / mind / quick
5 two / behaviour / faced
6 shoes / toed / open
7 rosy / child / cheeked
8 last / decision / minute
9 time / part / job
10 personality / going / easy

Your score /40

TEST 7 Compound nouns (1) noun + noun

7.1

10 marks

Find a noun that fits in the brackets to make two compound nouns. Use a dictionary if you need to.

Example: luxury (**goods**) train (*luxury goods* and *goods train* are both compound nouns)

1 junk (.....................) poisoning
2 address (.....................) token
3 cat (.....................) alarm
4 arms (.....................) relations
5 god (.....................) tongue

6 air (.....................) lights
7 junk (.....................) order
8 side (.....................) works
9 sea (.....................) screen
10 income (.....................) inspector

7.2

10 marks

Explain what the difference is between:

Example: generation gap and age gap   Generation gap refers to the differences in attitude etc. between different generations. Age gap refers to the difference in ages between, say, a brother and sister, or a husband and wife.

1 blood pressure and blood donor
2 kitchen scissors and nail scissors
3 sunglasses and wine glasses
4 pen-name and pen-knife
5 human being and human race

7.3

10 marks

Pair the words in the box to make ten compound nouns.

baby	birth	contact	effect	grass
greenhouse	holiday	hostel	control	lens
mark	opener	package	roots	sitter
fever	tin	trade	hay	youth

7.4

10 marks

Complete the blanks to make appropriate compound nouns.

Sam is an elderly business man. He had a heart (1)................................... last week when he was standing at a bus (2)................................... . He had been upset by a letter telling him that his bank (3)................................... was overdrawn and by newspaper articles which he had read that morning about plans to reinstate the death (4)................................... , to abolish the welfare (5)................................... and to ignore the abuse of human (6)................................... within the labour (7)................................... of his own country. The ambulance almost broke the sound (8)................................... getting him to hospital and it also almost had an accident as its windscreen (9)................................... were not working and it was raining hard. Fortunately, not all the medical staff of the hospital had joined the brain (10)................................... and he was quickly and effectively treated.

TEST
8 Compound nouns (2) verb + preposition

8.1

10 marks

Match the compound noun on the left with its meaning on the right.

1	breakout	a	prospect
2	breakthrough	b	reduction
3	check-out	c	strike
4	crackdown	d	major change
5	cutback	e	cash desk
6	drawback	f	escape
7	outlook	g	money passing through a company
8	shake-up	h	disadvantage
9	takeover	i	important discovery
10	turnover	j	purchase of one company by another one
11	walk-out	k	action to prevent something

8.2

10 marks

Add prepositions to complete the compound nouns in these sentences.

Example: They fixed a pin ....up......... of 'Boyzone' on the classroom wall.

1 At the end of his lecture on the effects of fall.............. the professor gave the students a print.............. with some shocking statistics.
2 The ....come of the strike was a shake.............. of personnel.
3 He says he became a drop.............. because of the break.............. of his parents' marriage.
4 Rapid staff turn.............. this year has led to a fall in the factory's ....put.
5 We went to a new factory ....let near the ....pass.

8.3

20 marks

Rewrite the sentences using compound nouns based on the phrasal verbs in the first sentence.

Example: The boss announced that he was cutting back on our budgets to a massive extent.
The boss announced *massive cutbacks in* our budgets.

1 It didn't surprise me when their marriage broke up.
The .... didn't surprise me.
2 Janet works out daily at the gym.
Janet does .... at the gym.
3 A surprising number of people turned out for the lecture.
There was a .... for the lecture.
4 Modern bosses usually ask workers to feed back on new initiatives.
Modern bosses usually ask workers for ....
5 John was there when the war broke out.
John was there at ....
6 Our travel plans were set back by the weather.
Our travel plans suffered ....
7 A tree that fell on the line held up trains all day.
A tree that fell on the line caused a .... all day.
8 The journalist wrote up the incident in an interesting way.
The journalist did ....
9 Our neighbour's house was broken into last night.
There was a .... last night.
10 Their new house is laid out in a very unusual way.
Their new house has ....

Your score

/40

TEST
9 Words from other languages

9.1
10 marks

Put the words in the box into the appropriate category:

Food	Clothes and materials	Society
bistro		

anorak	aubergine	~~bistro~~	caftan	coup	cuisine
gateau	ghetto	guerrilla	yashmak	yoghurt	

9.2
10 marks

Choose a word from the box that fits in each phrase.

avant-garde	blitz	chauffeur	confetti	crèche	cruise
cul de sac	fiasco	karate	siesta	~~theory~~	

Example: Einstein's ...theory... of relativity

1 to go on a luxury ....
2 to leave the baby in a ....
3 to have a .... after lunch
4 to live in a quiet ....
5 to have a .... on the housework

6 to take up ....
7 to throw ....
8 to employ a ....
9 the evening was a ....
10 .... art

9.3
10 marks

Match the names to the objects.

carafe	igloo	easel	cosmonaut	mosquito
duvet	shawl	tattoo	ski	mattress

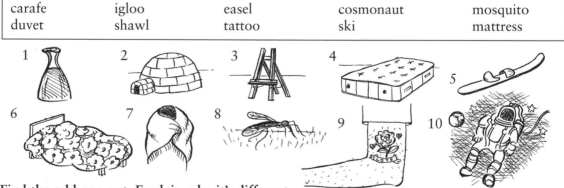

9.4
10 marks

Find the odd one out. Explain why it's different.

Example: (embargo) yacht ski snorkel the others relate to sport while embargo is a political and economic act

1 hippopotamus tycoon jackal lemming
2 ballerina judo soprano waltz
3 fjord patio steppe tundra
4 marmalade dachshund poodle rottweiler
5 bazaar boutique sauna kiosk

Your score
/40

10 Abbreviations and acronyms

10.1
10 marks

What do these abbreviations stand for?

Example: BBC   The British Broadcasting Corporation

1 The UN   5 Rd   8 ID
2 c/o   6 dep.   9 RSVP
3 asap   7 CD   10 arr.
4 MP

10.2
10 marks

What are the full forms of these shortened words?

Example: phone   telephone

1 lab   3 exam   5 ad
2 fridge   4 rep

What are the short forms of these full words?

Example: aeroplane   plane

6 newspaper   8 shoelaces   10 television
7 suitcase   9 wristwatch

10.3
10 marks

Here is a note written in a hurry, with a lot of abbreviations in it. Can you say what each one in bold means in full?

Example: tel   telephone

> To: John Furness
> From: Sally Oldbeck
>
> Dear John,
>
> Here are the times for my trip: **arr.** from Paris 2.25 **pm** at Victoria Station, **Wed** 14th. Stay with friends, **tel**: 41356787, address 56 Carlton **Ave**, Eastcheap, London S4. **Dep Sat** 17th from Heathrow, flight **no** EI 654 to Dublin.
> If you need to ring me in the office, it's *Oriental Imports **Ltd***, tel 3546659, **ext** 5656.
>
> Sally

10.4
10 marks

Use abbreviations instead of the words in bold.

Example: Mr S Williams, **care of** 76 North Street.   c/o 76 North Street

1 It is a digital camera, **that is to say** it doesn't use film, but takes pictures electronically.
2 I needed some paper, envelopes, pens, **and so on.**
3 There are several ways of solving the problem, **for example**, try fitting new batteries.
4 You can repair it yourself. **Please note**, the guarantee is no longer valid if you do.
5 She saw a **flying saucer or some kind of spaceship** in the sky above her house.
6 Her address is: Flat **number** 3, Block B, Horley **Street**, Bartsow. (*2 marks*)
7 She got a **Bachelor of Science degree** from London University, and now she's doing a **Doctor of Philosophy degree**. (*2 marks*)
8 There was a **postscript** at the end of the letter.

Your score
/40

11 New words in English

11.1 Match the words to the pictures.

10 marks

| mouse potato | in-line skating | teleshopping | road rage | audio book |
| snowboarding | cybercafé | surfing the net | video jockey | waitperson |

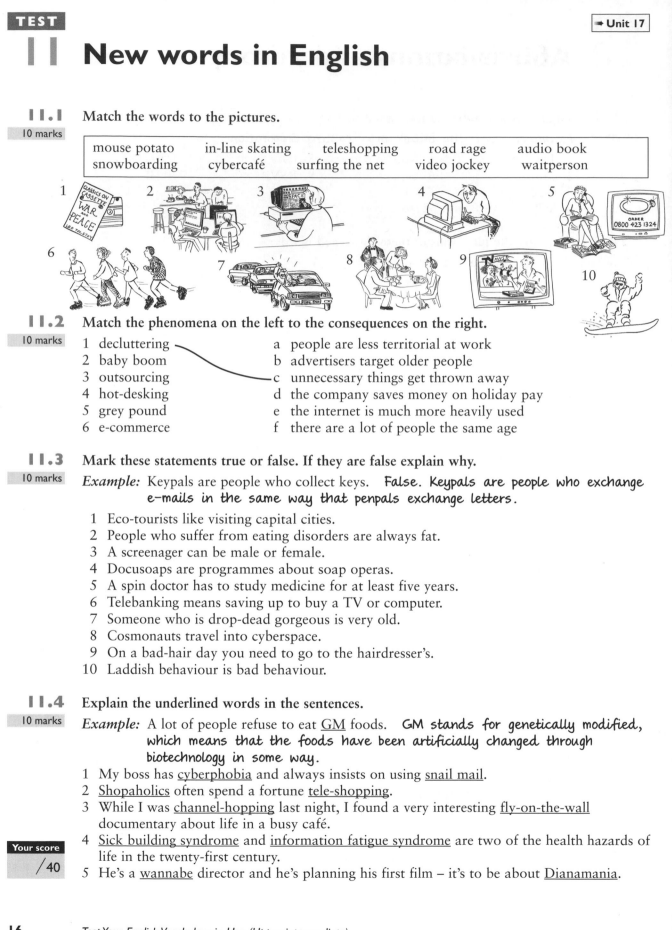

11.2 Match the phenomena on the left to the consequences on the right.

10 marks

1 decluttering   a people are less territorial at work
2 baby boom   b advertisers target older people
3 outsourcing   c unnecessary things get thrown away
4 hot-desking   d the company saves money on holiday pay
5 grey pound   e the internet is much more heavily used
6 e-commerce   f there are a lot of people the same age

11.3 Mark these statements true or false. If they are false explain why.

10 marks

Example: Keypals are people who collect keys.   *False. Keypals are people who exchange e-mails in the same way that penpals exchange letters.*

1 Eco-tourists like visiting capital cities.
2 People who suffer from eating disorders are always fat.
3 A screenager can be male or female.
4 Docusoaps are programmes about soap operas.
5 A spin doctor has to study medicine for at least five years.
6 Telebanking means saving up to buy a TV or computer.
7 Someone who is drop-dead gorgeous is very old.
8 Cosmonauts travel into cyberspace.
9 On a bad-hair day you need to go to the hairdresser's.
10 Laddish behaviour is bad behaviour.

11.4 Explain the underlined words in the sentences.

10 marks

Example: A lot of people refuse to eat <u>GM</u> foods.   *GM stands for genetically modified, which means that the foods have been artificially changed through biotechnology in some way.*

1 My boss has <u>cyberphobia</u> and always insists on using <u>snail mail</u>.
2 <u>Shopaholics</u> often spend a fortune <u>tele-shopping</u>.
3 While I was <u>channel-hopping</u> last night, I found a very interesting <u>fly-on-the-wall</u> documentary about life in a busy café.
4 <u>Sick building syndrome</u> and <u>information fatigue syndrome</u> are two of the health hazards of life in the twenty-first century.
5 He's a <u>wannabe</u> director and he's planning his first film – it's to be about <u>Dianamania</u>.

Your score

/40

TEST 12 Words commonly mispronounced

12.1
10 marks

These words are in the IPA. Write them in their normal spelling.

Example: /ˈɪntrəstɪŋ/ *interesting*

1 /daʊt/   3 /fɑːsən/   5 /hɪkʌp/   7 /niːl/   9 /ˈmʌsəl/
2 /plaʊ/   4 /ˈsəɪkɪk/   6 /resɪpiː/   8 /sɔːd/   10 /tʌf/

12.2
10 marks

Divide the words into pairs of words that rhyme.

Example: heard, word

arm	bend	blue	chalk	drove
dove	fiend	fork	friend	~~heard~~
hurry	leaned	lorry	love	palm
sorry	stove	though	through	
toe	~~word~~	worry		

12.3
10 marks

Mark the stressed syllable in the words in bold.

Example: Next week, we'll **pro<u>gress</u>** to the next stage.

1 What are your country's main **exports**?
2 They have **conflicting** ideas about their own roles.
3 The children have made a lot of **progress** with their maths.
4 The value of property usually **increases** every year.
5 Will they **permit** you to work here?
6 Although he is Russian, he has a UK permanent residence **permit**.
7 The highest July temperatures ever were **recorded** in London today.
8 I'll never **desert** you, the poet promised his love.
9 There is going to be an organised **protest** about the new by-pass.
10 What an **insult**! You have no right to speak to me like that!

12.4
10 marks

Underline all the silent letters in this text.

Julie, a friend I met at my psychology class, left the silver comb I gave her for Christmas in the castle when we spent an hour there last week. She took it out of her bag because she wanted to get some knots out of her hair while we were having a walk round the old tombs there. I told her she would lose it if she wasn't careful. And she did! Fortunately, an honest person picked it up and returned it to the gatekeeper. Julie feels very indebted to that anonymous person as she was very fond of that comb.

TEST

13 Onomatopoeic words

13.1

10 marks

Match the words (1–11) with the nouns (a–k) they collocate most closely with.

Example: 5a

1 clashing	7 peeping	a cows	g cymbals
2 creaking	8 sizzling	b propellers	h stairs
3 drizzling	9 spurting	c car horn	i bacon
4 grunting	10 tinkling	d horses	j rain
5 mooing	11 whirring	e fountain	k pigs
6 neighing		f bicycle bell	

13.2

10 marks

Circle the most appropriate word for each sentence.

Example: The dog always <u>whistles/clashes/(growls)</u> when it sees the postman.

1 Please can you help me <u>smash/mash/crash</u> the potatoes?
2 Children love <u>spraying/sputtering/splashing</u> through puddles.
3 She heard a <u>click/clank/clink</u> at the end of the phone as he hung up.
4 The wounded soldier <u>grunted/growled/groaned</u> in pain.
5 Do you hear those church bells <u>clinking/clanging/tinkling</u>?
6 She <u>sprayed/splashed/sprinkled</u> herbs on the fish and called the family to eat.
7 Sorry, I can't stop now. I've got to <u>whirr/dash/trickle</u>.
8 Can you <u>whistle/giggle/grumble</u> this song?
9 They <u>clanked/clinked/clashed</u> glasses and drank to the success of their project.
10 When she asked him to do the washing-up, he just <u>splashed/grunted/trickled</u>.

13.3

10 marks

Match these combinations of letters to their usual associations in English and give two examples of words for each letter combination.

1 gr-	movement of water	....
2 cl-	fast, violent movement	....
3 sp-	something light and repeated	....
4 wh-	something unpleasant or miserable	*growl, grumpy*
5 -ash	a sharp metallic sound	....
6 -ckle	movement of air	....

13.4

10 marks

Choose the verb from the side that best fits each gap.

Example: Camcorders ...*whirr*...... as the bridal couple emerge from the church.

1 The autumn leaves .... as I walk through them.
2 I .... with salt water if I have a sore throat.
3 Don't .... the ball so hard.
4 I hate it when fierce dogs ....
5 The attack left a .... in her arm.
6 Let's .... glasses and drink their health.
7 It's rude to .... in public places.
8 Horseriders carry a ....
9 People usually .... back when cows make a noise.
10 People with bronchitis tend to ....

clink
gargle
gash
growl
moo
rustle
spit
whack
wheeze
whip
~~whirr~~

Your score

/40

TEST

14 Homonyms

14.1

10 marks

Find five more examples of homophones (words that sound the same) and five more examples of homographs (words that are spelt the same) in the text. Explain why they are examples of homophones / homographs.

Examples: homophone: weight (wait)
homograph: sow (female pig) and sow (seeds)

Look at that fat sow! What a weight she must be! Heavier than lead! I've never seen anything like it. And there are two piglets underneath her. What a row they are making! If she rolls over on top of them, they won't live. They certainly need a big pen to house an animal like her!

14.2

10 marks

Find a word in the box that rhymes with the underlined words.

| choose | found | grinned | I've | juice |
| mooned | no | now | bed | nose | ~~seed~~ |

Example: Jane can be relied on to take the <u>lead</u>. ..seed..

1 The <u>wind</u> blew the tree down. ....
2 Have you <u>wound</u> the grandfather clock today? ....
3 I heard the band playing <u>live</u>. ....
4 Have you <u>read</u> Crime and Punishment? ....
5 I love your <u>bow</u> tie. ....
6 The children stood in two <u>rows</u>. ....
7 The cat just lay there after its operation licking its <u>wound</u>. ....
8 Do you <u>use</u> English Grammar in Use? ...., ...
9 At the end of the concert, the orchestra took a <u>bow</u>. ....

14.3

10 marks

Write each of these words, written in phonetics, in two different ways.

Example: /eə/ ..air, heir..

1 /grəʊn/ ....
2 /hɔːs/ ....
3 /taɪə/ ....
4 /waɪn/ ....
5 /peɪl/ ....
6 /əˈlaʊd/ ....
7 /piːl/ ....
8 /weɪst/ ....
9 /reɪn/ ....
10 /sɔːt/ ....

14.4

10 marks

Each of these book titles contains a pun (a joke based on words). Explain why these words are humorous.

Example: *What a Pane!,* a glassmaker's memoirs   What a pain! Meaning what a nuisance is a normal expression. Pane = a large piece of glass.

1 *Tee Time,* autobiography of a golf instructor.
2 *Love At First Site,* romance on an archaeological dig.
3 *Heaven Scent,* biography of a creator of perfumes.
4 *This Place has a Soul,* account of life in a fishmonger's.
5 *Sail of the Century,* account of a memorable voyage.

Your score

/40

TEST
15 Connecting and linking (1)

15.1
10 marks

Choose the correct alternative.

Example: I have to go to the hospital once a month now. ..*Previously*.. I had to go every two weeks.

      (a) Former   (b) Previously   (c) Prior

1 .... here, I used to work in a factory.
   (a) Before I've worked   (b) Before to work   (c) Before working
2 Take this umbrella just in case ....
   (a) of raining   (b) it will rain   (c) it rains
3 You can stay at our flat .... condition that you pay for your own phone calls.
   (a) of   (b) on   (c) in
4 You will get to the city centre .... bus you take.
   (a) however   (b) no matter   (c) whichever
5 My reason .... to go was that it was too far to drive.
   (a) of not wanting   (b) to not wanting   (c) for not wanting

15.2
6 marks

Fill the gaps using the words given.

throughout	supposing	owing to	providing	with a view to	unless

1 We sent out a questionnaire, ... finding out what people really wanted.
2 We shouldn't prepare the room .... we know definitely that she is coming.
3 .... the five years she was away, I never once stopped thinking of her.
4 It's OK to miss a few classes, ... you send a note to the teacher explaining why.
5 A lot of flights were late, ... the bad weather.
6 .... they don't give us the money. What then?

15.3
14 marks

Rewrite the sentences using the words in brackets.

Example: There were a lot of accidents as a result of the snow. (cause) **A lot of accidents were caused by the snow.** *or* **The snow caused a lot of accidents.**

1 Computers will change our lives even more in the new millennium. (bring about)
2 There was a 20% increase in taxes. Then there were serious riots and protests. (spark off)
3 He had made a mistake, and said so. (acknowledge)
4 The decision was unpopular and a lot of angry debate resulted. (give rise to)
5 A lack of communication between employers and employees causes this feeling of insecurity among the staff. (arise from)
6 Great changes in family life have come as a result of growing economic prosperity. (lead to)
7 A decision made ten years ago is responsible for the present problems. (stem from)

15.4
10 marks

Complete the missing words.

Example: I don't know what his mo..*tives*.. were for doing what he did.

1 Our plans have met all the con............... the authorities asked for.
2 I wonder what pr............... him to make such an aggressive comment?
3 The decision was the out............... of months of protests from environmental groups.
4 The entry re............... for this course are English and one foreign language.
5 I would not allow it under any cir............... .

Your score
/40

TEST

16 Connecting and linking (2)

16.1 **Complete the missing words.**

10 marks

1 He never works, and he wastes time and money. But fo........ al........ th........ , he is an old friend and so I will help him.
2 In a.............. t....... all her other talents, she is an excellent musician.
3 It would be silly to get it repaired. Af.............. al......., we're getting a new one next month.
4 Ad.............. , she was under great stress, but that is not an excuse for such bad behaviour.
5 George was wrong to send that letter, but eq.............. Jean was wrong to tell everyone.
6 The European Union was not happy with the plan. Fur.............. , there was a lot of opposition from Asian countries.
7 Ap.............. from doing a lot of sport, she also works in a children's home at weekends.
8 I don't think it's worth giving up so much time. Be.............. , it's very expensive.
9 I was looking for a holiday with a lot of excitement. Lik.............. , my brother wanted something very active, so we went snowboarding together.
10 Dear Sir/Madam, Fu.............. to my letter of 28/5, I am writing to ask whether …

16.2 **Replace the underlined word(s) with another version, as indicated in brackets.**

10 marks

Example: She plays the guitar. <u>Additionally</u>, she plays the piano. (more informal)
   And / What's more / In addition she plays the piano.

1 The flights get booked up very quickly. <u>Moreover</u>, we'll have to book before the 25th to get the cheap ticket. (more informal)
2 That shop sells pens, paper, you know, greetings cards, <u>etc.</u> (more informal)
3 She has an MA in economics. She has a diploma in politics <u>too</u>. (more formal)
4 It's always difficult to <u>say 'Yes, I was wrong.'</u> (more formal, use *admit*)
5 <u>OK, I may not understand</u> all the details, but I think I am right. (more formal, use *concede*)

16.3 **Fill the gaps with the correct prepositions.**

6 marks

Example: In addition ..*to*.. maths I'm doing a course in computer science.

1 He's a good athlete and an excellent musician .... boot.
2 We discussed the pollution in the river, along .... a few other local matters.
3 I broke my leg and Jim hurt his shoulder. .... top of all that we had to buy a new car.
4 Apart .... my other interests, I'm also keen on photography.
5 The weather was wet in September. .... the other hand, it was dry in October.
6 I wasn't offended when you called her a fool. .... the contrary, I was delighted.

16.4 **Correct the mistakes in these sentences.**

10 marks

Example: It's expensive. To the other hand, it's the only opportunity we'll get to go. **On the other hand, it's the only opportunity we'll get to go.**

1 He is a painter as well as he is a poet.
2 Likewise her brother went to university, and she did too.
3 So you do want to work. That's all good and well, but how are you going to find a job?
4 You need a good guide book. On addition, you need good equipment.
5 I'm not tired. Quite an opposite! I'm ready to work all night if necessary.

16.5 **Collocations. Match each word 1–4 with another word a–d.**

4 marks

Your score

/40

1 poles	a	discrepancy
2 world of	b	apart
3 huge	c	gap
4 yawning	d	difference

TEST 17 Text-referring words

17.1
10 marks

Complete each second sentence with one of the words in this list. There may be more than one correct answer.

| situation | dilemma | solution | approach | aspect |
| topic | position | question | issue | response |

1 TOM: Moving to London would mean a better job, but I'm worried about the children's education. They have such a good school here.
   MARY: Yes, it's a real .... We must think hard before we decide.

2 In future, cars will be taxed automatically as they enter the city centre. This new .... to the traffic problem may work, we shall just have to wait and see.

3 BABS: We talked about how trees communicate with one another through a sort of chemical language.
   ED: Trees communicating? That's a strange .... of conversation!

4 Thousands of people are hungry in the south of the country. The .... is getting worse every day.

5 Can we trust our politicians? This is a(n)...................... that is in the minds of many people nowadays.

6 Everyone knows that there is a crisis in the national health service. So far, however, there has been no .... from the Minister in charge.

7 ROGER: The new booking system really does seem to work.
   PAULA: Yes, I think we've found a .... at last.

8 I am convinced that Nancy should be dismissed. I am not prepared to change my .... on the matter.

9 MILDRED: So, is the real problem that there just isn't enough money to continue with the project?
   LARRY: Well, it's one .... of the problem, but there are other difficulties too.

10 The Prime Minister spoke about the need to reduce unemployment. She said this was the biggest .... facing the government at the moment.

17.2
10 marks

In each of these pairs of sentences, the *same* word fits the gap. What is it? You are given the first letter.

Example: (a) The s.ubject...... of his speech was world peace.

          (b) She did not want to talk about her illness so we changed the s.ubject...... .

1 (a) She made an interesting p...................... about the need for real changes in the way we do things.
   (b) Well, even though I don't think we should over-react, I do see your p...................... .

2 (a) What is the p...................... with regard to new members? Are they allowed to vote?
   (b) I think her p...................... in relation to whether we should sell up or not is totally mistaken.

3 (a) I personally don't care whether she is appointed or not. But I think the boss expects me to take a v...................... on the matter.
   (b) So you really think we should just cancel the whole programme? That's quite a radical v...................... . I don't think many people will agree with you.

4 (a) The k...................... to the problem of poor communications is to spend more on technology.

(b) We've talked and talked, but we still can't find a k...................... to solving the dilemma.

5 (a) One reporter suggested that an official at the Ministry was corrupt, but the Minister rejected this c...................... .

(b) The c...................... that protests have been ignored is not true. Everyone has a voice.

17.3

5 marks

Add the correct prepositions.

1 There is no way .... the situation.
2 D'you think we'll find a solution .... the problem?
3 What was her reaction .... the claim that it was her fault?
4 Your judgement .... the situation is a bit naive, if I may say so.
5 What is your attitude .... the issue of private versus public schools?

17.4

10 marks

Match the headlines with the extracts from the stories.

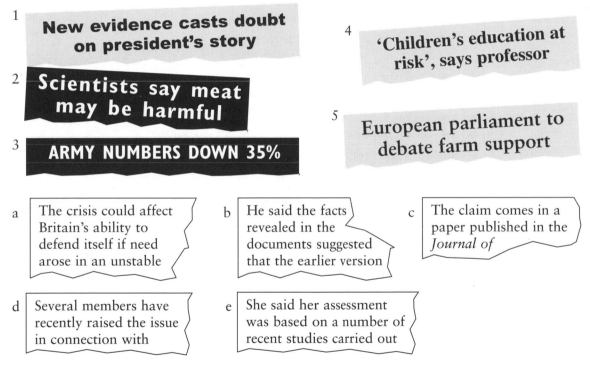

1 **New evidence casts doubt on president's story**

2 **Scientists say meat may be harmful**

3 **ARMY NUMBERS DOWN 35%**

4 **'Children's education at risk', says professor**

5 **European parliament to debate farm support**

a The crisis could affect Britain's ability to defend itself if need arose in an unstable

b He said the facts revealed in the documents suggested that the earlier version

c The claim comes in a paper published in the *Journal of*

d Several members have recently raised the issue in connection with

e She said her assessment was based on a number of recent studies carried out

17.5

5 marks

State whether the sentences are *a fact, a claim, a reaction* or *a belief*.

Example: There will be life after death. **a belief**

1 Why should I do it? Why can't someone else do it?
2 Without oxygen, human beings cannot live.
3 The Minister was not telling the truth when he said more money would be granted next year.
4 Love can overcome any difficulty in life.
5 President Kennedy died in 1963.

Your score

/40

TEST
18 Discourse markers in speech

18.1

10 marks

Use these markers to fill the gaps.

mind you	let me see	now then	look	well
so	great	hang on	you see	OK

1 A: What's Sally's last name?
  B: Oh, ... , I know it begins with B, erm, Barlow, I think.
2 A: D'you live in the centre of town?
  B: .... , near the centre, but not actually in it.
3 A: Why weren't you here to meet her?
  B: I got mixed up. .... , I thought she was coming Wednesday.
4 (*Teacher to the class*) .... , listen to this tape, and answer the questions.
5 A: Edna wants you to ring her about the –
  B: Edna! I don't want to talk to her!
  A: .... ! Let me finish! She says it's good news.
  B: .... , you know I don't like her. Why didn't you just say I was away?
  A: Why should I tell stories for you?
6 A: That's all for today, then.
  B: Yes. .... , see you tomorrow?
  A: .... , same time tomorrow.
  B: ....
7 A: It's warm today, isn't it?
  B: Yes. .... , it is the beginning of spring, so we shouldn't be surprised.

18.2

15 marks

Choose the best alternative, (a), (b) or (c) to fill the gaps.

1 A: She's always annoying me.
  B: (a) Fine (b) Well then (c) Right, you should tell her!
2 A: I just don't know what to do.
  B: (a) Sort of (b) You know (c) Listen, I've got an idea …
3 A: What's the matter with you?
  B: Oh, I guess I'm (a) hold on (b) sort of (c) well then, worried about my exams.
4 A: Here's a package for you.
  B: (a) Right (b) You know (c) Sort of, leave it on the desk, will you, please.
5 A: Could you give me Jim's e-mail address?
  B: Yes, (a) fine (b) anyway (c) hold on, I'll just have to get my address-book.
6 A: So that's what you think we should do, is it?
  B: Yes, (a) anyway (b) at the end of the day (c) mind you, I'll ring you later and we can make a final decision then.
7 A: They'll be here at about 5.30.
  B: (a) Fine (b) Hold on (c) Still, I'll be here waiting for them.
8 A: What's the matter?
  B: It's oh, (a) right (b) you know (c) anyway, the same old problem.
9 A: There seems to be nothing we can do about it.
  B: Well (a) for instance (b) at the end of the day (c) well then, we just have to accept it.

10 A: I'm very sorry I missed Peter yesterday when he was here.
   B: Yes. (a) Sort of (b) At the end of the day (c) Still, you'll get another chance. He's coming again next Wednesday.

11 A: She's not very friendly, is she?
   B: Why? What do you mean?
   A: Well (a) still (b) for instance (c) fine, she never says hello if you meet her in the corridor.

12 (*B is talking to* C)
   A: Sorry to interrupt. Have you got the time?
   B: Yes, ten to six. So, (a) where was I (b) still (c) at the end of the day, oh yes, I was going to give you my address.
   C: Yes, please.

13 A: Well, why not come with us?
   B: Well, a you're leaving too early, (a) and so (b) and well then (c) and b, there are already four of you. It's only a small car.

14 A: What happened?
   B: Tracy (a) I mean (b) so (c) listen, Sandra forgot to bring the tickets.

15 A: Hey, what happened with Barbara and the student from Taiwan?
   B: Well, (a) fine (b) where was I (c) where shall I start, it was about three weeks ago I think. Barbara was just going out of …

18.3

5 marks

Match the words in the left hand column with those on the right to make discourse markers.

1 well   you
2 hang   then
3 mind   see
4 now   on
5 you   then

18.4

10 marks

Complete the markers.

1 When you want to get back to what you were talking about, you can say 'Where .... ?'
2 When you want to summarise or conclude something, you can say 'At the .... '.
3 When you want to get a group of people's attention to tell them something important, you can say '................... then!'
4 When you don't want to be too precise, you can say '................... of'.
5 When you want to explain or clariy something, you can say 'You ....'.

TEST
19 Discourse markers in writing

19.1

10 marks

Use discourse markers to rewrite the beginnings of these sentences, without changing the meaning. The first letter of the discourse marker is given.

Example: *As a last point*, let us consider the effect on the environment. F..*inally*.. ...

1 *The first point is*, we should not allow our personal feelings to influence our decision. F.....................

2 *Now changing the subject* to the question of violence on television, the evidence for its effects are not clear. T.....................

3 *As a side issue, not part of the main question*, there was a similar example in 1984, but that is not important in the present argument. In p.....................

4 *To end this argument*, we may say that it is too early to decide what will happen to the economy as a result. In c.....................

5 *To continue*, let us consider the situation of children who only have one parent. N.....................

6 *While not discussing any further* the question of social consequences, there are important political reasons why the government will not support the idea. L..................... a.....................

7 *To say again briefly what I have already said*, there are three main arguments. To s..................... u.....................

8 *As argument number three*, let us look at the history of the problem since 1995. T.....................

9 *Put in a very short way*, there are two objections to the plan that need to be considered. B.....................

10 *As argument number two*, people need to feel that their opinions are listened to. S.....................

19.2

22 marks

Answer the questions.

Example: *Say* can be used to mean 'for example': True or false? **True**

1 Give *two* other ways of saying the discourse marker *first*.
.... (*4 marks*)

2 Which is correct as another way of saying the discourse marker *finally*? *At last* or *lastly*? (*2 marks*)

3 Give another way of saying *in conclusion*. (*2 marks*)

4 Give *two* other ways of saying the discourse marker *to sum up*.
.... (*4 marks*)

5 Which of the two answers in 4 is more formal? (*2 marks*)

6 Give another way of saying *for example*. (*2 marks*)

7 Give another way of saying *on the other side of this page*. (*2 marks*)

8 *So to speak* and *as it were* mean more or less the same: True or false? (*2 marks*)

9 *In other words* and *that is to say* are similar in meaning, but *in other words* is less formal: True or false? (*2 marks*)

Test Your English Vocabulary in Use (Upper-intermediate)

19.3 Fill the gaps.

8 marks

SUNSEEKER HOLIDAYS

Wyndham Precinct
Langtown

Mr Bill Berry
72 Corbally Mansions
Clifton

18.4.2000

Dear Mr Berry,

With (1)r........................... to your letter of 13th April 2000 requesting a refund for your travel tickets, I should like to make the (2)f........................... points:

- The rules do not permit cancellation of booking less than three days before departure (3)(s........................... the enclosed leaflet, paragraph 6.6).

- In an (4)e........................... letter to you (dated 2nd January 2000), we alerted you to the penalties for late cancellation.

- The company is not obliged to refund the cost of travel even if there are strong personal reasons for cancellation. You should contact your insurance company (for (5)f........................... information please read paragraph 8.5 of the enclosed leaflet).

- May I (6)r........................... you also to the conditions as printed on the form which you filled in at the time of making the booking? You will see there that the conditions were quite clear.

As I mentioned (7)a..........................., cancellation less than three days before departure means you do not have the right to a refund. In (8)o........................... words, despite the circumstances you describe, there is nothing that we can do to help, and the matter must now rest with your insurance company.

Yours sincerely,

I. Coldheart

Ivor Coldheart (Mr)
Managing Director

Your score

/40

TEST
20 Uncountable words

20.1
10 marks

Are these nouns normally countable or uncountable? Tick (✔) the correct box.

		countable	uncountable
1	passport	☐	☐
2	currency	☐	☐
3	luggage	☐	☐
4	reservation	☐	☐
5	accommodation	☐	☐
6	flight	☐	☐
7	information	☐	☐
8	travel	☐	☐
9	visa	☐	☐
10	journey	☐	☐

20.2
10 marks

Correct the mistakes in these sentences.

1 We're going to the shops tomorrow. I want to look at some new furnitures, Dan needs new clothes, Maria wants to look at skiing equipments and Sheila needs some papers for her computer printer. We'll probably spend lots of moneys!

2 After some courses, he found that he was making progresses and increasing his knowledges of geography. He looked forward to continuing his studies at university and, perhaps, one day, doing some advanced researches into the geography of his local area.

3 I really need some advices from you before I take up the violin. Do you have any tips about buying an instrument? Are there any works by famous composers that are easy for a beginner? Which kinds of musics would you recommend? Any informations you can give me would be useful.

20.3
10 marks

Which ten of these food names are not normally used in the plural?

flour	carrot	loaf	fish	cooking-oil	fruit	toast	pancake
garlic	biscuit	parsley	soya-sauce	rice	wheat		

20.4
10 marks

Complete the sentences with these words connected with materials and resources. Decide whether the word is used countably or uncountably.

stone	leather	coals	cloth	plastic	glass

1 Most of the cottages were built of .... , which was not surprising because you could see large .... lying everywhere in the fields around the village.

2 I have some .... here which I bought to make a dress. I hate it now. I think I'll tear it up and make some .... for dirty jobs in the kitchen.

3 .... can produce a phenomenal heat. That's why I find it hard to believe that he said he once saw someone in India walking over red-hot ....

4 The car seats are all .... They're much more comfortable than ....

5 The .... that those wine-..................... are made of is very pure and expensive.

Your score
/40

TEST
21 Words that occur only in the plural

21.1

10 marks

Ten of these nouns are normally only used in the plural. Which ones? Tick (✓) the boxes.

1 binoculars ☐
2 trousers ☐
3 slippers ☐
4 pants ☐
5 sunglasses ☐
6 gloves ☐
7 tongs ☐
8 tweezers ☐
9 corkscrews ☐
10 e-mails ☐
11 headquarters ☐
12 pyjamas ☐
13 shears ☐
14 rulers ☐
15 swimming trunks ☐

21.2

10 marks

Fill in the gap with a plural word that means the same as the words in brackets. The first letter is given.

Example: Her luggage was searched by the ...*customs*.... . (officials at the airport or port)

1 The a............................. in the concert hall are excellent. (the sound quality)
2 We complained to the a............................. but it was a waste of time. (the people in power)
3 The c............................. of each chapter are listed at the beginning of the book. (what is in it)
4 A dangerous criminal has escaped. The police have no idea of his w............................. . (where he is)
5 Some of the g............................. on the lorry were damaged in the accident. (things to be bought and sold)

21.3

10 marks

Identify the objects in these pictures.

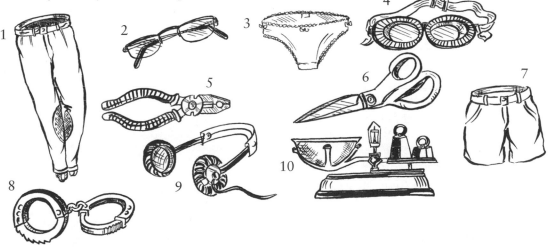

21.4

10 marks

Make the verbs and pronouns singular or plural, as appropriate.

Example: Physics (be) a very difficult subject. **Physics is a very difficult subject.**

1 Darts (be) a good game if you are bored and just want to have fun.
2 Economics (be) my best subject when I was at school. Maths (be) compulsory and I hated (it/them).
3 The news (be) very bad, I'm afraid. Do you want to hear (it/them)?
4 The spaghetti (be) ready. I hope you're hungry, because there (be) a lot of (it/them).
5 Looks (be) not the most important thing. What matters is a person's personality.

TEST
22 Countable and uncountable nouns with different meanings

22.1
10 marks

Decide whether the noun in brackets should be used countably (with the indefinite article *a* or in the plural) or uncountably (no *a* or no plural).

Example: Would you like ...cheese.... in your sandwich? (cheese)
('A cheese' usually means a big, whole round cheese.)

1 There was .... on the floor and I got a little piece in my foot. (glass)
2 I bought some .... to make a dress for our Patsy's wedding. (cloth)
3 Would you like .... ? My sister bought me a big box for my birthday. (chocolate)
4 Would you prefer .... or .... for dinner tonight? (fish/chicken)
5 Could I borrow .... ? My shirt is creased through being in the suitcase for two days. (iron)
6 There's .... at the back of the house. We could go for a walk there after lunch if you like. The trees are lovely right now. (wood)
7 As I arrived I saw .... walking around in the garden. And that was in the middle of the city! (chicken)
8 Did you buy .... for the computer? I want to print something. (paper)
9 We need some .... for the orange juice. Could you fetch some? (glass)

22.2
10 marks

Say whether the nouns can be singular (S), plural (P), or both (S/P) in these sentences. Put the verb 'be' in the correct form.

Example: We don't use so much/many paper(s) since we started using e-mail.
(S) – singular. (The material you write letters on is 'paper'.)

1 After the dog had been on it, there (be) hair(s) all over the sofa.
2 The economic (policy/policies) of this government (be) completely crazy.
3 I love meeting (people) from different countries and different professions.
4 He wanted to build six houses, so he bought (land) just on the edge of the city.
5 She bought me a wonderful gift: *The Complete (Work) of Shakespeare* on CD-ROM.

22.3
10 marks

What's the difference between ...?

1 *pepper* and *a pepper*?
2 *tape* and *a tape*?
3 *rubber* and *a rubber*?
4 *coffee* and *a coffee*?
5 *trade* and *a trade*?

22.4
10 marks

What do we normally mean when we use the following nouns?

1 peoples (in the plural)
2 a home (with *a*)
3 lands (in the plural)
4 iron (without *an*)
5 a paper (with *a*)

Your score
/40

TEST
23 Collective nouns

23.1
10 marks
Fill the gaps with collective nouns in the correct form, singular or plural. Use each noun once only.

| gang | crowd | pack | herd | team | deck | shoal | flock | group | swarm |

1 There was a .... of sheep in one field and a .... of cows in the next field.
2 The boat had a glass bottom and we could see .... of beautifully-coloured fish.
3 She was attacked by a .... of bees and had to go to hospital.
4 .... of hungry dogs wandered through the streets looking in rubbish bins for food.
5 A .... of thieves had broken in and stolen jewellery and paintings worth
£1 million. A .... of detectives is now on the scene looking for evidence.
6 There was a large .... of people, waving banners and protesting. There were about
500 people there. A small .... of police officers was trying to hold them back.
7 Have you got a .... of cards? I've learnt a new game. It's fun.

23.2
10 marks
Describe the pictures using these collective nouns. Use each one once only. Number 1 uses two words.

| set | row | range | stack | clump | pair |

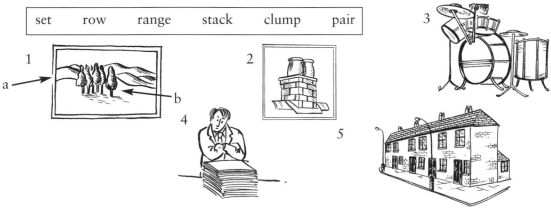

23.3
10 marks
Use a collective noun to express the same meaning as the underlined words.

Example: The <u>people who played together in the match</u> were congratulated by the captain.
The team were congratulated by the captain.

1 The <u>people who work in this company</u> are mostly young people.
2 The <u>people who flew the plane</u> remained calm during the emergency landing.
3 The <u>people who acted in the film</u> were just ordinary people, not famous stars.
4 The <u>people in general</u> have a right to know how the politicians are spending their taxes.
5 The <u>people who act in this theatre</u> are on strike, so there will be no performances this week.

23.4
10 marks
Use collective nouns. What could you call ...?

Example: a lot of goats in one field **A herd of goats.**

1 six tables neatly on top of one another
2 flowers wrapped in nice paper, as a present
3 lots of dirty clothes on the floor
4 six wine glasses all exactly the same
5 hundreds of strong complaints

6 a lot of untrue claims or allegations
7 questions asked one after another
8 a large group of elephants
9 a large group of birds
10 a group of wolves

Your score
/40

TEST
24 Making uncountable nouns countable

24.1
10 marks

Choose words from the box to fit into the sentences. Make the words plural, if necessary.

article	breath	carton	gust	loaf
lump	means	puff	spot	stroke

Example: Put another ...lump...... of coal on the fire.

1 Jo spends all day in the library but I don't believe she does a .... of work there.
2 It's very stuffy here. I'm dying for a .... of fresh air.
3 How many .... of sugar would you like in your coffee?
4 Customers are permitted to take up to six .... of clothing into the fitting room.
5 When I was walking home, I felt the first .... of rain and soon it was pouring.
6 He took the cigarette out of his mouth and blew out .... of smoke.
7 The donkey is the main .... of transport on the island.
8 A sudden .... of wind blew my papers all over the garden.
9 I'd like two .... of bread, please, and a .... of milk.

24.2
10 marks

What do each of these pictures show?

Example: two cartons of milk

24.3
12 marks

Write an expression using *a state of* + one of the abstract nouns from the box to complete the sentences.

agitation	~~anxiety~~	confusion	disrepair	emergency	flux	uncertainty

Example: John's in ..a state of anxiety... waiting for his exam results.

1 After the floods .... was declared in the city.
2 After the Revolution, the country was in ....
3 The old school building needs renovation as it is in ....
4 When the lights went out, everyone ran around in... .
5 Fiona is still in .... as to whether she has got the job.
6 Gran got herself into .... , as she thought I'd had an accident.

24.4
8 marks

Rewrite the text, making all the uncountable nouns countable.

Example: You can travel round England using different transport.   *You can travel round England, using different means of transport.*

Your score

/40

Before visiting England, let me give you some advice and some information. Don't take too much luggage with you but take some warm clothing. You never know whether you are going to get good weather or not. One day you have thunder, lightning and rain, the next it is sunny.

TEST

25 Containers and contents

25.1 Name the following items.

10 marks

Example: 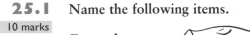 a tube

25.2 Explain the difference between each of the two phrases.

20 marks

Example: a barrel of beer / a can of beer A barrel of beer is a large wooden or plastic container holding many gallons (50 litres or more) of beer whereas a can is a metal container typically holding half a litre.

1 a bottle of milk / a crate of milk
2 flowers in a pot / flowers in a tub
3 a packet of cigarettes / a carton of cigarettes
4 a tube of paint / a tin of paint
5 a shopping bag / a shopping basket
6 a bowl of ice-cream / a tub of ice-cream
7 a cup of tea / a mug of tea
8 a pot of ointment / a tube of ointment
9 a box of sweets / a jar of sweets
10 a jewellery box / a jewellery case

25.3 Put the words from the box into the correct column.

10 marks

chocolates	crayons	honey	instant coffee	jam
matches	olives	~~paper clips~~	pins	tea bags	tools

a box of	a jar of
paper clips	

Your score

/40

TEST

26 Countries, nationalities and languages

26.1

10 marks

Make nationality/cultural identity adjectives from these nouns and put them into the correct group. *Example:* Turkey *Turkish (group A)*

| Japan | Brazil | Ireland | Israel | Ukraine |
| Arabia | Iraq | Denmark | Portugal | Iceland |

group A: -ish adjectives   group C: -(i)an adjectives   group E: -ese adjectives
group B: -ic adjectives   group D: -i adjectives

26.2

10 marks

The nouns change spelling and/or stress and/or pronunciation when they are made into adjectives. Write the adjective and explain the changes.

noun	adjective	change
Israel	Israeli	stress changes from Israel to Israeli
Peru		
Canada		
Norway		
Egypt		
Italy		

26.3

5 marks

Make a noun meaning 'a person from that country or geographical region'.

Example: Denmark *a Dane*

1 The Arabian Gulf countries   4 Sweden
2 Britain   5 Spain
3 Finland

26.4

5 marks

Correct the mistakes in these sentences.

Example: She went to the Russia on holiday. *She went to Russia (no 'the')*

1 I think she married a Scottish.
2 Have you ever heard Bulgarish music? It's really wonderful.
3 He went to work in the Centre East, in Jordan, I think.
4 I would like to live in UK for a while to improve my English.
5 I love the colour of the Mediterrane sea.

26.5

10 marks

What do we call …?

1 A person who speaks two languages perfectly?
2 The different ways of speaking in one and the same language?
3 The language you learnt from your birth?
4 The country whose capital is Manila?
5 The national language of the Netherlands?

Your score

/40

TEST
27 The weather

27.1

10 marks

Put these words into the *cold, hot,* or *wet/dry* column, as appropriate.

frost	stifling	drought	chilly	scorching	freezing
downpour	close	~~rainy~~	flood	heatwave	

cold	hot	wet/dry
		rainy

27.2

10 marks

What do we call …? The first letter is given.

Example: A light that flashes in the sky during a storm?   l.*ightning*...............

1 Deep piles of snow blown by the wind?   s...............................
2 Snow and rain mixed together?   s...............................
3 A heavy snowstorm with high winds?   b...............................
4 Dirty, brownish, melting snow in the streets?   s...............................
5 Very light, fine rain?   d...............................
6 Rain that only lasts a very short time?   s...............................
7 Little balls of ice that fall from the sky?   h...............................
8 Thunder and heavy rain at the same time?   t...............................
9 A very light fog?   m...............................
10 Fog and smoke/pollution together?   s...............................

27.3

16 marks

Fill the gaps. The first letter is given. One mark per gap.

1 In the spring the ice m...................... , the ground t...................... and plants start to grow again.
2 Normally, at that time of year, the weather is very cold, but that day it was very m...................... , with a temperature of 12 degrees and sunshine.
3 It snowed last night but it didn't s...................... , so the roads are clear.
4 As I looked out to sea, the horizon was h...................... , and the sky and sea seemed to be one blue mass.
5 It was hot on the beach, but there was a gentle b...................... that cooled us a little.
6 The sky was very o...................... , and then it p...................... down.
7 It was a b...................... hot day, but it was also extremely h...................... , which made us sweat, so all we could do all day was sit inside with the air conditioning on.
8 There was a violent s...................... last week. There was t...................... rain all day and all night, and the streets got f...................... .
9 The north is usually cold and d...................... , while the south is warmer and very dry.
10 The weather was rather m...................... that day, and I found it difficult to concentrate on my work. I just wanted to fall asleep all the time.
11 There was h...................... and rain falling at the same time, and all the garden was white for just a few minutes.

27.4

5 marks

Put these words on a scale from 'strong' to 'weak'.

gale   breeze   blustery winds   hurricane

Your score

/40

TEST 28 Describing people: appearance

28.1
10 marks

Fill the gaps to describe the people in these pictures. The first letter is given.

1 He's b..................... , and d.....................-skinned.
2 She's got b..................... hair and is f.....................-skinned.
3 She's got l..................... , c..................... hair.
4 He's got a beard and a m..................... and a slightly c..................... face.
5 She's got long, s..................... hair and is t.....................-faced.

28.2
30 marks

Answer the questions. You are sometimes given the first letter of the missing word.

1 What is the adjective form of the word *waves* when it refers to a person's hair?
2 What do we call the small, pale brown spots some people have on their skin, especially fair-skinned people? f.........................
3 Give an adjective that means a person has red or reddish hair. g.........................
4 What colour is auburn? Is it 'golden, reddish-brown' or is it 'very dark, almost black'?
5 If someone has a *crew cut*, is their hair long or short?
6 Is *stout* similar in meaning to (a) *slim* or (b) *plump*?
7 What is a polite word that means 'fat'. o.........................
8 If someone is stocky, they are rather thin. Is this true or false?
9 If someone is anorexic, they are usually very thin indeed. Is this true or false?
10 What word means 'extremely fat'? o.........................
11 If a person is *scruffy*, is that normally a positive or a negative thing?
12 Which is more negative, to call someone *slim* or *skinny*?
13 How do we describe someone who is losing their hair at the front of their head? We say 'His/her hair is r......................... '.
14 What does it mean to say that someone has a *healthy complexion*? Is it that their face and skin look healthy or that just their eyes look healthy?
15 What should you remember about the adjective *handsome*?

Your score
/40

TEST 29 Describing people: character

29.1
10 marks

Match each adjective (1–11) with its synonym or near-synonym (a–k).

1 half-witted   a gregarious
2 impolite   b curt
3 inward-looking   c down-to-earth
4 quarrelsome   d sly
5 sensible   e stubborn
6 obstinate   f dim
7 brusque   g bright
8 cunning   h introverted
9 smart   i reliable
10 trustworthy   j discourteous
11 sociable   k argumentative

29.2
10 marks

Which people does the speaker approve of and which does the speaker not approve of?

Example: Jack's miserly but Jill is generous.
The speaker doesn't approve of Jack but does approve of Jill.

1 Sam is broad-minded and Sue is original.
2 Mark is arrogant and Mary is curt.
3 John is pushy but Jane is assertive.
4 Amos is inquisitive and Anna is naive.
5 Dave's pig-headed and Debby's brusque.

29.3
10 marks

Rewrite the sentences in exercise 29.2. Use adjectives from the box to show that this speaker has a different opinion about whether the people's characteristics are positive or negative.

ambitious	bossy	determined	~~extravagant~~	frank	innocent
inquiring	open	self-assured	~~thrifty~~	unprincipled	weird

Example: I don't agree. I think Jack is thrifty and Jill is extravagant.

29.4
10 marks

Match the adjectives in the box to the people who are being described.

jealous	~~optimistic~~	sincere	eccentric	gifted	relaxed
envious	sensitive	cruel	nosy	easy-going	

Example: optimistic – Jill always sees the bright side of things.

1 Robert always wants what other people have got.
2 Sandra plays the piano better than anyone else I know.
3 Beth takes everything in her stride and never gets upset.
4 Paul seems to enjoy pulling his cat's tail.
5 Dan doesn't mind what we do when we stay at his place.
6 You always know that Clare means what she says.
7 Julie felt terrible when her boyfriend left her for someone else.
8 Becky only ever wears black clothes and black lipstick.
9 Whenever we have visitors, our neighbour Fred is at his window watching who it is.
10 Emma always gets very upset if she feels that she is being criticised or laughed at.

Your score
/40

TEST
30 Relationships

30.1 Say whether these statements are true or false. Tick (✔) the boxes.

10 marks

Example: A 'colleague' means someone I share a house or a flat with.

	True	False
Example: A 'colleague' means someone I share a house or a flat with.	☐	✔
1 'An acquaintance of mine' means 'someone I work with'.	☐	☐
2 'Workmate' is less formal than 'colleague'.	☐	☐
3 'Husband/wife-to-be' is often seen in newspapers.	☐	☐
4 'Partner' means someone you are in business with, not someone you live with.	☐	☐
5 'To worship' and 'to idolise' can mean 'to like or love somebody very much indeed'.	☐	☐
6 A steady boy/girlfriend is just a casual, occasional relationship.	☐	☐
7 If you fancy someone, you find them attractive.	☐	☐
8 'To look up to someone' is the opposite of 'to look down on someone'.	☐	☐
9 If you feel repelled by someone, you find them attractive.	☐	☐
10 If you despise someone, you don't like or respect them at all.	☐	☐

30.2 Rewrite the sentences using an appropriate form of the word in brackets.

10 marks

Example: Lily is not Tom's girlfriend any more. (ex-) **Lily is Tom's ex-girlfriend.**

1 Jason and I study together and go to the same classes. (-mate)
2 I'm sorry, I dislike Nancy intensely. (stand)
3 They live together but they are not married. (partner)
4 She's had a lot of arguments with her colleagues again. (fall out)
5 I think Richard is in a relationship with his best friend's wife. (affair)

30.3 Fill the gaps. The first letter is given.

10 marks

1 I g............... on with all my workmates, and we have a lot of fun.
2 Lucy and I just don't see e............... to e............... when it comes to politics.
3 I hate it when we argue. Couldn't we try to make it u............... and be friends again?
4 She's senior t............... me in the office, so I have to do what she tells me.
5 I may be old-fashioned but I think children should respect their e............... .
6 I felt strongly r............... by his unpleasant attitude. I never want to speak to him again.
7 I heard that Brian and Fiona have s............... up. I thought they were madly in love.
8 He's not really a friend, just a casual a........................ .
9 He doesn't just love her, he absolutely i........................ her!
10 Jill is David's f............... . They plan to get married next year, as far as I know.

30.4 Change the words underlined to give the sentences the *opposite* meaning.

10 marks

Example: I <u>like</u> people who smoke in public places. **I hate people who smoke.**

1 I <u>respect</u> my boss, even though most of my colleagues feel the opposite.
2 Maria's his <u>current</u> girlfriend. He has so many and changes them so often it's difficult to know who is who.
3 He's <u>senior</u> to her in terms of length of service, so the promotion is not surprising.
4 I <u>loathe</u> people who devote their whole life to working and studying.
5 She's <u>not a particularly special</u> friend of mine.

Your score

/40

TEST

31 At home

31.1

10 marks

Label the rooms and other features on this house-plan. The first letter is given.

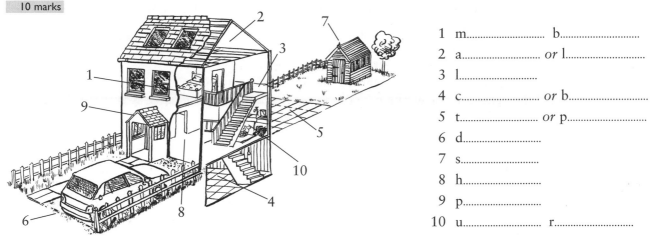

1 m............................ b............................
2 a............................ *or* l............................
3 l............................
4 c............................ *or* b............................
5 t............................ *or* p............................
6 d............................
7 s............................
8 h............................
9 p............................
10 u............................ r............................

31.2

10 marks

Answer the questions.

Example: What do we call the flat area at the top of the stairs in a house? **the landing**

1 What could you use to change the TV channel without moving from your chair?
2 What do we call a large cupboard or small room you can walk into, where food is stored?
3 What do you call a bedroom mostly for guests who come to stay?
4 What's the difference between a 'cellar' and a 'basement'?
5 Where would you find the 'loft' or 'attic'?
6 What do we call a room used for reading/writing/studying?
7 What do we call something you can put under a dinner-plate to protect the table surface?
8 If you want to iron clothes, what is the thing you need most, apart from an iron?
9 What could you use to protect the kitchen work-surface if you wanted to cut vegetables?
10 What do you look for if you want to plug in your hair-dryer in a hotel room?

31.3

10 marks

Answer the questions.

Example: What would you use a tea-towel for? **Drying dishes**

1 When would you need a dust-pan and brush?
2 What are bin-liners for?
3 What's a corkscrew for?
4 In which room would you be most likely to find a grater, and what is it for?
5 Is a coaster a person who lives near the coast? Explain your answer.

31.4

10 marks

Answer the questions.

1 Explain the difference between, (a) a detached house, (b) a semi-detached one and (c) a terraced one. (*3 marks*)
2 Explain what a 'bedsit' is. (*2 marks*)
3 Explain how a 'bungalow' is different from other types of house. (*1 mark*)
4 Explain what it means to have a 'self-contained' flat. (*2 marks*)
5 Explain the difference between (a) a cottage and (b) a villa. (*2 marks*)

Your score

/40

TEST
32 Everyday problems

32.1

10 marks

Rewrite these sentences using the words and phrases given.

Example: There's water coming from this pipe. *This pipe is leaking.*

power cut	flood	break down	come off	run out	~~leak~~

1 I can't open the door; the handle is lying on the floor.
2 The bathroom was full of water this morning. It was terrible.
3 All the lights are not working.
4 The batteries are not working in my Walkman.
5 Our washing machine stopped working last week.

32.2

10 marks

Put a tick in the box for the most likely collocations.

	leaking	chipped	dented	stained	bruised
car bumper					
water-pipe					
forehead					
dinner-plate					
tablecloth					

32.3

20 marks

Answer the questions. You are sometimes given the first letter of the missing word.

1 What's the difference between a cut and a graze?
2 Which is more serious, twisting your ankle or breaking it?
3 What's another way of saying that the water will not run away in a sink or washbasin? The sink/washbasin is b............................ .
4 Why might you run to the kitchen to get a cloth? Somebody has s............................ some milk or something.
5 Why might you ring your flatmate from a phone box and ask him/her to meet you outside the flat with his/her keys? Because you are l............................ o............... .
6 Would you be pleased if your car had a flat battery? Explain.
7 If your watch was fast, would you be likely to arrive too early or too late for an appointment?
8 What is a more polite/indirect way of telling someone you *lost* a letter they sent you? – I'm sorry, I m............................ your letter.
9 If your clock is slow, do you need to turn the hands forward or back?
10 Can you say 'I banged my head' or 'I bumped my head' with more or less the same meaning?

Your score

/40

TEST
33 Global problems

33.1
10 marks

Choose the correct answer, (a), (b) or (c).

1 A volcano <u>erodes / erupts / erases</u>.
2 An epidemic <u>spreads / sprouts / sprays</u>.
3 War can <u>break up / break through / break out</u>.
4 A hurricane can <u>swerve / sweep / swipe</u> across an area.
5 An earthquake can <u>quake / rake / shake</u> a city.
6 People who have no food may <u>strive / starve / hunger</u> to death.
7 It was a very bad accident. There were 150 <u>causalities / casualities / casualties</u>.
8 Thousands of children were <u>victims / victors / victories</u> of the civil war.
9 Only ten people <u>surveyed / revived / survived</u> the accident.
10 Thousands of <u>refusees / refugees / rescuees</u> are living in emergency camps.

33.2
16 marks

Fill the gaps. The first letter is given.

1 This area has s...................... many droughts this century.
2 Several buildings were d...................... in the bomb blast, but, fortunately, nobody was
   i...................... since the police had cleared the area before the bomb exploded.
3 The farmers' crops have failed for the third year in a row. It now seems certain that there
   will be severe f...................... unless food can be brought in from the outside.
4 A t...................... can be so powerful that it can lift a car up and spin it round and round in
   the air.
5 This region has seen many d...................... in recent years, including an earthquake, floods,
   and a hurricane.
6 After the battle, the d...................... were buried and the w...................... were taken to a military
   hospital.

33.3
14 marks

Give the name of ... (The first letter is given.)

1 a disease that can be caught by a bite from a cat, dog or fox that has it. R *abies* ....
2 a disease associated with a colour as part of its name. Y.................... f....................
3 a disease that can be caught from a bite from a mosquito. M....................
4 a terrible skin disease that leaves the skin deformed. L....................
5 two diseases often caught by consuming infected food or water. C.................... and
   t....................
6 a disease that has spread throughout the world since the 1980s. A....................

Your score
/40

TEST
34 Education

34.1 The words in the box refer to types of education in Great Britain. Group them according to
10 marks the age at which people go through them, starting when they are little children.

| junior school | college | comprehensive | play-school | grammar school |
| secondary | university | primary | nursery | sixth form | further |

2–5 years old	5–12/13 years old	12/13–18 years old	18+ years old
	junior school		

34.2 True or false. Tick (✔) the correct box.

8 marks

	True	False
1 In Britain, if you say, 'She went to a public school', you mean a private school.	☐	☐
2 Degrees can be obtained from schools, colleges or universities.	☐	☐
3 If you are a postgraduate student, you have normally already done your first degree.	☐	☐
4 To enter a 'grammar school' in Britain, you normally have to pass an exam.	☐	☐
5 In Britain, A-levels are normally taken at 16 years old.	☐	☐
6 Teachers at schools and universities are called 'professors'.	☐	☐
7 In a university, a tutorial usually has fewer students than a seminar.	☐	☐
8 In Britain, 'junior school' means school for children under five.	☐	☐

34.3 Fill the gaps. The first letter is given.

10 marks

1 I failed my exam first time round, so I'm going to r..................... it next month.
2 I've got to d..................... an exam next week, so I'll be r..................... every evening till then.
3 BEN: Hi, did you p..................... your geography exam?
   LORNA: Yeah, I did quite well in fact, I got 76%.
   BEN: Oh well done! So they give you a per cent? I thought they gave g..................... .
   LORNA: Yeah, they give you both. Mine was an 'A'. So how about you?
   BEN: Well, we don't have exams, we have c..................... a..................... , so you just have to
          do coursework, and you get a m..................... for each essay.
4 MEG: Why did you s..................... classes yesterday?
   ED: Don't tell anyone, but I was out till 3.30 the night before, so I just stayed in bed
          all day.
5 I d..................... well in my exams. I was pleased, and so were my parents.

34.4 Give a word or phrase that means the following. The first letter of each word is given.

12 marks

1 The age at which children normally leave school for good. s..............-l.............. a.......
2 Money given by the government which enables a person to study. g..............
3 A school run and funded by the government. s.............. s..............
4 A university teacher who is not a professor. Give two names. l.............. or t..............
5 Classes that people can go to after work. e..................... c..............

Your score
/40

Test Your English Vocabulary in Use (Upper-intermediate)

TEST

35 Work

35.1

10 marks

Complete the words. The first letter is given.

Example: S_ales_ a_ssistant_: Sells goods to the public.

1 U.............. r.............. : Looks after the interests of staff/workers, for example in getting better pay and conditions.
2 R.............. : Sits in the lobby or entrance area of a company. Greets and checks in visitors.
3 D.............. : Very senior person. Sits on the board of the company.
4 P.............. o.............. : Takes care of filling vacant posts. Is responsible for general matters concerning staff/employees.
5 S.............. o.............. : Makes sure there are no dangers from machines, etc., and that accidents at work are properly investigated.
6 E.............. : An expert in financial matters.
7 L.............. : Does very hard, physical work.
8 S.............. w.............. : Does specific tasks that he/she is trained for (e.g. assembling a TV set).
9 S.............. : Makes sure everyone knows their job and is doing it properly.
10 A.............. : Looks after the day-to-day organisation of the company.

35.2

7 marks

Match the words on the left with words that collocate with them on the right.

1 Get		a early retirement
2 Earn		b a responsibility
3 Apply for		c the sack
4 Take on		d shift-work
5 Do		e nine-to-five
6 Be made		f a living
7 Work		g a job
8 Take		h redundant

35.3

13 marks

Are these jobs (a) a profession, (b) unskilled work or (c) a trade.

1 an electrician
2 an office cleaner
3 an architect
4 a lecturer
5 a carpenter
6 a school caretaker
7 a receptionist
8 a plumber
9 a lawyer
10 checkout assistant
11 a dentist
12 a newspaper seller
13 a publisher

35.4

5 marks

Explain the following.

1 shift work
2 flexi-time
3 maternity leave
4 on strike
5 promotion

35.5

5 marks

What's wrong with these sentences? Correct them.

Example: I was laid off, so I have a job now.
 I was laid off, so I don't have a job now.

1 She's a workaholic; she hates going to work every day.
2 I feel very well, so I'm on sick leave.
3 I got laid off from my job at the factory, so I still work there.
4 You're so good at your job we've decided to fire you.
5 Bill's wife has just had a baby, so he's on maternity leave.

Your score

/40

36 Sport

36.1 Name the sports in these pictures.

6 marks → 14 marks

36.2 **What do you hold in your hand when you are …?**

6 marks

Example: doing archery?   **A bow and arrow**

1 playing tennis?   3 fishing?   5 playing hockey?
2 playing golf?   4 playing baseball?   6 playing pool or billiards?

36.3 **Fill the gaps.**

10 marks

1 Italy beat Sweden .... three goals in the final.
2 He .... the record in 1992 and has .... it ever since. No-one can beat him.
3 How many points has your team .... this season?
4 MALCOLM: Have you .... swimming? I haven't seen you at the pool recently.
   BRIAN: Yeah, I got bored with it. I've .... golf instead.
5 Our team has never been .... in the last ten years. We've won every game.
6 Who's running the first leg in the .... ?

36.4 **What do we call …?**

10 marks

1 a person who runs very long races (e.g. 5000 metres, marathons)?
2 a person who runs fast over short distances (e.g. 100 metres)?
3 a person who just runs round their neighbourhood every morning to keep fit?
4 the thing you hold in your hand when you row a boat?
5 a person who plays tennis?
6 a person who plays cricket? Give *two* ways of saying it.
7 a person who does archery?
8 what you hold in your hands in a canoe?
9 a person who does gymnastics?
10 a person who climbs mountains?

Your score
/40

TEST

37 The arts

37.1

10 marks

Sort these words into three columns.

| country and western | fiction | opera | ceramics | sculpture |
| biography | rock | poetry | painting | ballet | novel |

performing arts	literature	fine arts
country and western		

37.2

7 marks

Put the definite article *the* where it is necessary. Leave the gap blank if it is not necessary.

1 The government is increasing the amount of money it gives every year to .... arts.
2 She was trained in .... ballet and .... modern dance.
3 We've got some tickets for .... theatre. Would you like to come with us?
4 .... art of writing a biography is to try to imagine the world in which the person lived.
5 I prefer .... modern poetry; it's easier to read than the classics.
6 He was very good at .... art at school. Now he works as a book illustrator.

37.3

10 marks

Choose the correct answer of the choices underlined.

We went to see a new [(1)]produce/production/producing of *Romeo and Juliet* last week. The [(2)]sceneries/sights/sets were very atmospheric and realistic and the [(3)]costumes/suits/dresses were wonderful, with a good [(4)]persons/list/cast, and the [(5)]actions/acting/acts was excellent. Cerise O'Donnell [(6)]put/took/gave a marvellous [(7)]performance./show./play. It [(8)]did/took/got some [(9)]brave/rave/crave [(10)]recences/reprieves/reviews in the papers the day after.

37.4

13 marks

Answer the questions or fill in the gaps.

1 What's .... the opera house next week? (*2 marks*)
2 Our local cinema is .... a James Bond film all this week. (*1 mark*)
3 Which of the arts are these associated with?
   (a) a beautiful, hand-painted china vase. (*1 mark*)
   (b) a newly-designed shopping centre. (*1 mark*)
   (c) a water-colour. (*1 mark*)
4 Where in a newspaper would you look for a review of a new play? (*1 mark*)
5 What do we call a person who likes art very much? (*1 mark*)
6 NINA: I've just bought a new e............... of the complete works of Shakespeare.
   BOB: Oh, yes. Who p............... it? (*2 marks*)
7 Have you seen the e............... of paintings by Picasso in the City Gallery? (*1 mark*)
8 RORY: Who did that fabulous new piece of s............... in the main square?
   FRAN: Oh, it's by a Norwegian s............... called Erik Fossberg. (*2 marks*)

Your score

/40

TEST

38 Music

38.1
10 marks

Match the word on the left to its definition on the right.

1 album
2 arrangement
3 backing
4 cassette
5 chord
6 hit
7 hum
8 muzak
9 scale
10 single
11 whistle

a individually released song
b music supporting the lead singer
c sing a tune with lips closed
d notes going up at equal intervals
e CD with a number of tracks
f make sound by blowing air through lips
g particular adaptation of a piece of music
h very successful song
i three or four notes played together
j recorded light music played in public places
k magnetic tape you can record on

38.2
10 marks

Can you identify what these styles of music are? Each dash indicates a missing letter.

Example: p __ p **pop**

1 j __ __ z
2 b __ __ __ s
3 f __ __ k
4 c __ __ __ __ __ y
5 s __ __ l

6 r __ __ k
7 c __ __ __ __ __ __ __ l
8 o __ __ __ a
9 d __ __ __ o
10 h __ __ __ y m __ __ __ l

38.3
10 marks

Which is the odd one out in these words and expressions relating to music and why?

Example: guitar, piano, violin, harp *The piano is the only one that does not have strings that you can see.*

1 contemporary music, electronic music, seventies music, 20th century music
2 soothing, relaxing, discordant, tuneful
3 orchestral music, chamber music, big band music, rock music
4 background music, soundtrack, contemporary music, dance music
5 jazz, blues, muzak, heavy metal

38.4
10 marks

For each of the words find (a) a near synonym and (b) an antonym from the words in the box.

Example: innovative: **synonym = creative; antonym = unoriginal**

background	classical	~~creative~~	discordant	loud	modern
relaxing	rousing	serious	soft	tuneful	~~unoriginal~~

1 deafening   2 soothing   3 light   4 tuneless   5 contemporary

39 Food

39.1

10 marks

Divide these words into meat, fish, and vegetables.

~~carrot~~	aubergine	cod	veal	mutton	plaice
cauliflower	spinach	venison	salmon	onion	

meat	fish	vegetables
		carrot

39.2

10 marks

Match the words on the left with the examples/definitions on the right.

1	bitter	a	a lot of sugar
2	sour	b	no flavour at all
3	hot, spicy	c	far too much sugar
4	sweet	d	has a good taste/flavour
5	bland	e	e.g. fruit which is not ripe
6	salty	f	like a beautiful, ripe strawberry
7	sugary	g	sharp/unpleasant
8	sickly	h	e.g. a strong Indian curry
9	savoury	i	a lot of salt
10	tasty	j	rather negative, very little flavour
11	tasteless	k	pleasant, slightly salty or with herbs

39.3

10 marks

Match the names with the pictures.

garlic	kiwi fruit	grapes	melon	broccoli
leeks	pear	mushrooms	strawberries	pineapple

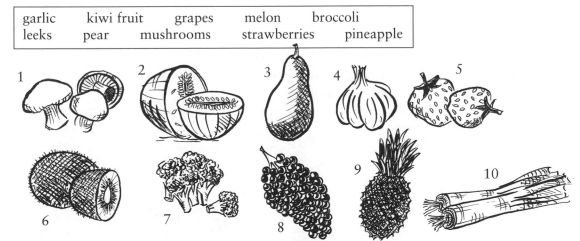

39.4

10 marks

Give a word that means …

1 a dish you have after the main course, for example, ice-cream.
2 very heavy and hard to digest (begins with *s*).
3 cooked with heat coming from above (for example, for a sausage or burger).
4 cooked in the oven, with a little fat or oil (for example, for a whole chicken).
5 that something is not cooked enough.

Your score

/40

TEST 40 The environment

40.1
10 marks

What word matches these definitions? The first letter is given in brackets.

Example: A valley with steep sides. ..Gorge......

1 A very large sea. (o)
2 Land with sea on all sides. (i)
3 Where a river meets the sea. (m)
4 A river that flows into another river. (t)
5 Where a river starts. (s)

6 A river of ice. (g)
7 The top of a mountain. (s)
8 Where land meets sea very steeply. (c)
9 A small stream. (b)
10 Land with sea on 3 sides. (p)

40.2
10 marks

What are each of these natural features? Which of them need *the*?

Example: Seychelles. **group of islands, The Seychelles.**

1 Andes
2 Kilimanjaro
3 Hungary
4 Gulf Stream
5 Amazon
6 Atlantic
7 Tasmania
8 United Arab Emirates
9 Loch Ness
10 Baltic

40.3
10 marks

Use the words in the box to complete this text about environmental problems.

conditions	destruction	disposal	farming	greenhouse	heavily
layer	over-fishing	over-populated	~~polluted~~	resources	

Pollution is a major problem of our times. Air, water and land are all _polluted_ . Poor waste
(1)............... is to blame for many of the problems and the situation is particularly acute in (2)...............
industrialised and (3)............... regions. Pollution of the atmosphere has led to the destruction of the
ozone (4)............... and to the (5)............... effect. Other environmental problems have been caused by
too rapid a use of (6)............... . There are far fewer fish in the sea because of (7)............... and the
(8)............... of the rainforests is having unforeseen ecological consequences. Battery (9)...............
provides a lot of food but involves keeping animals in unnatural and unhealthy (10)............... .

40.4
5 marks

What are the opposites of the adjectives below?

1 a deep river
2 a gentle slope
3 a rocky beach
4 a rough sea
5 an extinct volcano

40.5
5 marks

Name these things.

Example: ..A bay........

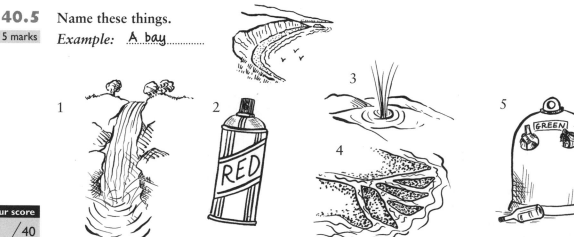

Your score
/40

TEST
41 Towns

41.1
10 marks

Here are some facilities which are often found in towns. Write the word which completes the name of the place.

Example: railway ...station.....

1 swimming ....
2 art ....
3 opera ....
4 radio ....
5 registry ....

6 department ....
7 law ....
8 golf ....
9 taxi ....
10 skating ....

41.2
10 marks

Name the odd one out in each set and explain why it is odd.

Example: bus stop, petrol station, taxi rank, railway station   Petrol station – you can catch public transport at each of the other places but at the petrol station you buy petrol for your car.

1 youth hostel, B&B, police station, hotel
2 disco, rush hour, traffic jam, commuting
3 citizens' advice bureau, job centre, department store, health centre
4 catering, vandalism, crime, pollution
5 housing estate, slums, parking meter, residential district

41.3
10 marks

Choose a word in the box and put it in the right form to fit each gap. (Note that half of the words need to be put into a different form.)

bustle	cathedral	fame	harbour	industry	large
lie	~~major~~	market	picturesque	populate	

Aberdeen is a ...major... city in the north-east of Scotland with a (1)................ of nearly 200,000. It is the (2)................ city in the Highlands. It (3)................ between the Rivers Dee and Don and its impressive (4)................ has been used by fishing boats for centuries. The fish (5)................ is still (6)................ early in the morning but Aberdeen is now more (7)................ as the centre of the North Sea oil (8)................. The old part of the town is (9)................ with its narrow streets leading to an ancient (10)................ and one of the oldest universities in Britain.

41.4
10 marks

Match the place on the left with what happens there on the right.

1 adult education centre
2 bottle bank
3 chemist's
4 concert hall
5 estate agency
6 harbour
7 job centre
8 library
9 suburbs
10 take-away
11 town hall

a prescriptions are made up
b boats are tied up
c music is played to audiences
d houses are bought and sold
e local government meetings are held
f people live there rather than in the centre
g books are borrowed
h evening classes take place
i cooked food is bought to eat at home
j people try to find work there
k glass is left for recycling

Your score
/40

TEST
42 The natural world

42.1
10 marks

Label the pictures. Choose from the words in the box.

bark	bat	beak	branch	frog	hedgehog
hoof	~~mane~~	nest	snail	trunk	

Example: mane

1 ....
2 ....
3 ....
4 ....
5 ....
6 ....
7 ....
8 ....
9 ....
10 ....

42.2
15 marks

Name the odd one out. Explain why it is the odd one out.

Example: pigeon, bat, peacock, eagle   A bat is a mammal but pigeons, peacocks and eagles are birds.

1 scales, bough, gills, tail
2 worm, fir, oak, elm
3 whiskers, paw, claws, wing
4 crab, shark, twig, whale
5 seal, stalk, petals, pollen

42.3
5 marks

Put these verbs in the right places.

fertilise	flower	harvest	pick	plant

First farmers (1)................. their crops. Then they (2)................. them. When the crops are ready for eating or processing, the farmers (3)................. them. Gardeners usually like to grow things that (4).................. In spring or summer, they may (5)................. them to make their home look beautiful.

42.4
10 marks

Answer these questions.

Example: Is a pine tree deciduous or evergreen?   Evergreen

1 Is an oak deciduous or evergreen?
2 Do frogs hibernate?
3 Is a snail a mammal?
4 Are dinosaurs extinct?
5 What tree is traditionally decorated at Christmas time?
6 What popular sweet-smelling flower with sharp thorns is a symbol of love?
7 Does a worm make honey?
8 Which animal lives in the desert and has two humps?
9 What does a cat use its whiskers for?
10 Which bird has a particularly magnificent tail which it can open out to display beautiful colours?

Your score
/40

TEST

43 Clothes

43.1
10 marks

Label these pictures. Use the words in the box.

cardigan	coat	collar	cuff	dressing gown
hem	mittens	sleeve	slippers	waist

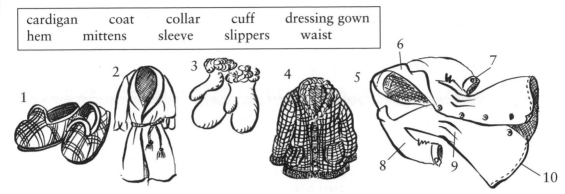

43.2
10 marks

Fill in the gaps in this text with *on, of, up, out, in, down*.

I went shopping for clothes yesterday and tried ...on... lots of different things. I've grown [1]............
[2]............ my old winter coat so first I put [3]............ a coat that I liked but it was too long. It
needed taking [4]............ . It was also a bit loose and needed taking [5]............ as well. So, then I tried
a different style but that was too short and too tight. It needed letting [6]............ and letting
[7]............ . So I changed [8]............ [9]............ that and decided to go for a party dress instead. I love
dressing [10]............ for parties.

43.3
8 marks

Divide these words into two groups – those that have positive and those that have negative
associations.

chic	elegant	fashionable	messy	old-fashioned
scruffy	smart	trendy	~~well-dressed~~	

positive	negative
well-dressed	

43.4
12 marks

Answer these questions.

checked	flowery	pin-striped	plain	spotted	striped	tartan

1 What are these patterns called? Label the
drawings with the appropriate names from
the box.
2 What can buckles and laces both be used for?
3 What are belts and braces used for?
4 What are heels and soles both parts of?
5 Where do we get wool and leather from?

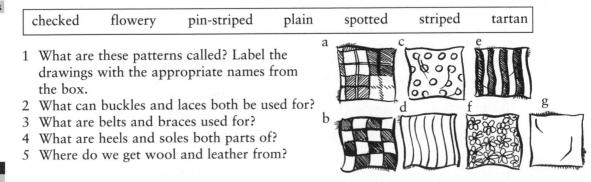

TEST
44 Health and medicine

44.1

10 marks

Fill in the missing words in these sentences. Use words from the box.

bandage	black	blisters	bruises	hypochondriac
indigestion	operation	prescribe	rest	round	~~sore~~

Example: I think I'm getting flu. I've got a dreadful ...sore.... throat.

1 A ball hit him in the face and gave him a terrible .... eye.
2 Doctors .... medicine to treat their patients.
3 Paul is having an .... today – they're taking his wisdom teeth out.
4 The doctor says I've just got a bug that's going ....
5 We'll get the nurse to put a .... on your ankle.
6 The best thing for her would be total bed .... for a few days.
7 I'm covered in .... after playing rugby.
8 My new shoes are too tight – I've got .... on my heel.
9 Don't eat so fast – you'll get ....
10 He's always imagining he's ill – he's a dreadful ....

44.2

10 marks

Label the pictures. The first letters are given to help you.

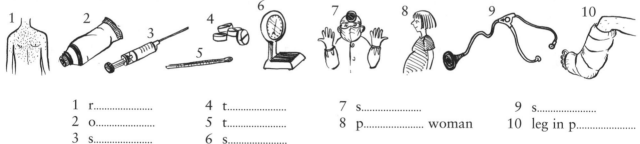

1 r...................	4 t...................	7 s...................	9 s...................
2 o...................	5 t...................	8 p................... woman	10 leg in p...................
3 s...................	6 s...................		

44.3

10 marks

Put these illnesses in the correct category – Infectious or Non-infectious.

~~allergy~~	brain haemorrhage	cancer	chickenpox	flu	heart attack
mumps	rheumatism	sore throat	sprained ankle	ulcer	

Infectious: ....

Non-Infectious: ...allergy..

44.4

10 marks

Make collocations by matching a word from box A with a word from box B.

Example: 1e swollen glands

A
1 ~~swollen~~	7 raised
2 operating	8 painful
3 lung	9 blood
4 heart	10 food
5 brain	11 itchy
6 health	

B
a allergy	g nose
b cancer	h theatre
c temperature	i haemorrhage
d insurance	j joints
e ~~glands~~	k attack
f pressure	

Your score

/40

TEST
45 Travel

45.1 **Which is the odd one out? Explain why.**

10 marks

Example: to be stranded, <u>to take off</u>, to be delayed, to be wrecked   *take off is a normal action for a plane whereas the other verbs suggest a travel crisis of some kind*

1 docker   helicopter   steward   captain
2 cockpit   steering wheel   nose   wings
3 engine-room   joystick   bridge   deck
4 liner   ferry   jet   yacht
5 to swerve   to overtake   to drive   to land

45.2 **Look at the drawings. Find the names for these things in the word square.**

10 marks

G	E	A	R	S	T	A	M	T	O
A	R	N	S	T	A	I	L	O	S
N	E	R	Y	I	R	D	N	D	T
G	O	P	A	G	E	B	U	O	Y
P	P	O	C	K	I	O	B	N	R
L	I	G	H	T	H	O	U	S	E
A	L	U	T	A	I	T	F	O	S
N	O	A	W	Z	L	E	F	I	N
K	T	R	P	A	D	O	E	F	Y
H	A	D	E	R	S	A	T	Y	E

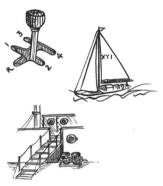

45.3 **What is the word that matches each of these definitions? Choose from the words in the box.**

10 marks

aisle	back	brakes	bunk	~~cabin~~	flight
crew	overtake	runway	starboard	supersonic	

Example: a bedroom on a ship   *cabin*

1 a bed in a ship
2 people who work on a ship
3 a journey by air
4 use these to stop a car
5 corridor in a plane

6 travelling faster than sound
7 track where planes land and take off
8 right on a boat (not left)
9 to pass another car
10 another word meaning reverse a car

45.4 **There are six mistakes in this text. Underline them and then correct them. The first one has been done for you as an example.**

10 marks

Last year my uncle went on a very interesting <u>travel</u> in South America. He took a fly to Chile. There was fog when the plane arrived to the airport and the driver found it very difficult to land. Eventually, he succeeded and the voyagers all got off and went into the airport. A lot of them had to exchange planes there.

journey – travel never takes a

Your score
/ 40

TEST
46 Holidays

46.1 Find the holiday word or expression from the box that matches each description below.

10 marks

Example: canvas or nylon structure that you pitch and then sleep in **tent**

1 almost everything is paid for in advance
2 place where you sleep and have breakfast but no evening meal
3 buying an annual right to holiday accommodation for part of the year
4 place where you can pitch your tent to sleep in
5 holiday on a ship calling in at different ports
6 simple, cheap accommodation aimed largely at young people
7 a convenient way of taking your own holiday accommodation with you and parking it where you wish
8 you rent a flat or house and do your own cooking and cleaning
9 a simple hotel, usually family-run
10 a place offering accommodation and lots of entertainment and activities for all generations

| B & B | camp-site | caravan | cruise | guesthouse | holiday camp |
| package holiday | self-catering | tent | timeshare | youth hostel | |

46.2 Match these holiday brochure words on the left with their synonyms on the right.

10 marks

1	breath-taking	a	famous
2	exhilarating	b	luxurious
3	exotic	c	natural
4	glamorous	d	heavenly
5	legendary	e	unrivalled
6	mighty	f	stunning
7	picturesque	g	unusual
8	sublime	h	invigorating
9	unspoilt	i	powerful
10	unsurpassed	j	pretty

46.3 Which adjective collocates better with the following nouns?

10 marks

1 river – mighty or exclusive?
2 climb – breath-taking or exhilarating?
3 view – stunning or luxurious?
4 restaurant – glamorous or intoxicating?
5 village – mighty or picturesque?
6 opportunity – unsurpassed or picturesque?
7 location – intoxicating or exotic?
8 hospitality – breath-taking or legendary?
9 charm – picturesque or luxurious?
10 night-club – unspoilt or exclusive?

46.4 Use the clues to solve the crossword.

10 marks

Across

1 Small house in the mountains or in a holiday camp
2 Take your trunks or costume here
4 Big Ben, Buckingham Palace and the Tower of London are some of the most famous ones in London
6 You do this with your tent (or you play football on it)
7 Bed on top of another one (e.g. on ship)
8 Small, not too expensive hotel

Down

1 Place to put your tent or caravan
2 People like doing this on the beach
3 Ski slope
5 You can enjoy looking at this in the countryside

Your score

/40

TEST 47 Numbers and shapes

47.1
10 marks

Write these numerical expressions in words.

Example: $2 \times 2 = 4$ Two times two equals four

1   $32°F = 0°C$
2   36.8%
3   $15.4 = 15\frac{2}{5}$
4   $56 \div 7 = 8 + 41 - 3 = 46$
5   $2^4 = 4^2$

47.2
10 marks

Which is which?

1   a square and a triangle

2   a circle and an oval

3   the radius of a circle and its circumference

4   a cube and a sphere

5   an octagon and a pentagon

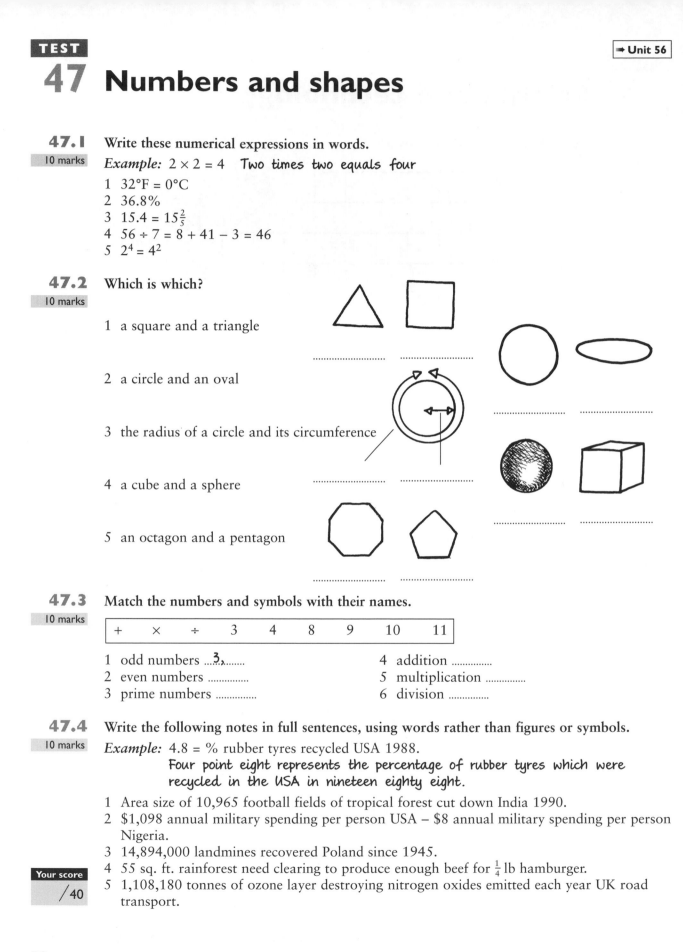

47.3
10 marks

Match the numbers and symbols with their names.

+	×	÷	3	4	8	9	10	11

1   odd numbers ...**3**,.......
2   even numbers ....
3   prime numbers ....

4   addition ....
5   multiplication ....
6   division ....

47.4
10 marks

Write the following notes in full sentences, using words rather than figures or symbols.

Example: 4.8 = % rubber tyres recycled USA 1988.
Four point eight represents the percentage of rubber tyres which were recycled in the USA in nineteen eighty eight.

1   Area size of 10,965 football fields of tropical forest cut down India 1990.
2   $1,098 annual military spending per person USA – $8 annual military spending per person Nigeria.
3   14,894,000 landmines recovered Poland since 1945.
4   55 sq. ft. rainforest need clearing to produce enough beef for $\frac{1}{4}$ lb hamburger.
5   1,108,180 tonnes of ozone layer destroying nitrogen oxides emitted each year UK road transport.

Your score
/40

TEST
48 Science and technology

48.1

10 marks

Name these modern inventions.

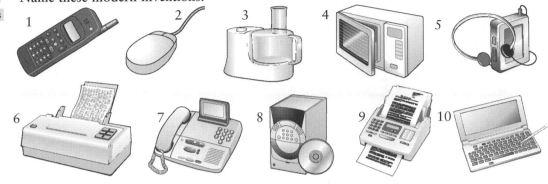

1 2 3 4 5

6 7 8 9 10

48.2

16 marks

Complete this table.

Science	Subject of study	Scientist
genetic engineering	manipulation of DNA	genetic engineer
molecular biology		
bioclimatology		
astrophysics		
cybernetics		
information technology		
ergonomics		
genetics		
civil engineering		

48.3

14 marks

Complete the sentence by forming a word from the root in brackets at the end of the sentence. Use a dictionary if you need to.

Example: When you have finished your ...**dissection**... please turn to page 55. (dissect)

1 I came to the .... that the theory was incorrect. (conclude)
2 Researchers must first make a careful .... of the problem. (analyse)
3 Fleming was responsible for the .... of penicillin. (discover)
4 The .... of the earth on its axis causes night and day. (rotate)
5 The .... of these two gases can be dangerous. (combine)
6 The scientist carried out many .... (experiment)
7 Joe is a systems .... (analyse)
8 We owe a great deal to the .... of the steam engine. (invent)
9 The .... of the steam engine was James Watt. (invent)
10 You must take out a .... on this idea. (patent)
11 There was a violent .... when the chemical was added. (react)
12 Scientists have to .... (theory)
13 They also have to .... (hypothesis)
14 Don't forget to switch on the video .... (record)

Your score

/40

Computers and the Internet

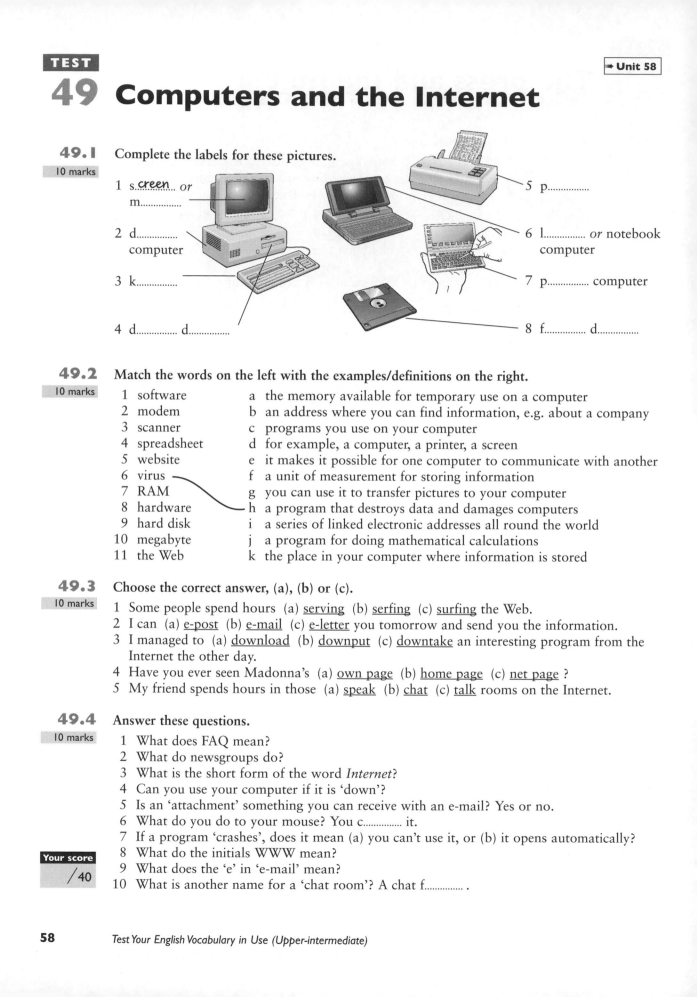

49.1 Complete the labels for these pictures.

10 marks

1 s.creen.. *or*
  m..............

2 d..............
  computer

3 k..............

4 d.............. d..............

5 p..............

6 l.............. *or* notebook
  computer

7 p.............. computer

8 f.............. d..............

49.2 Match the words on the left with the examples/definitions on the right.

10 marks

1	software	a	the memory available for temporary use on a computer
2	modem	b	an address where you can find information, e.g. about a company
3	scanner	c	programs you use on your computer
4	spreadsheet	d	for example, a computer, a printer, a screen
5	website	e	it makes it possible for one computer to communicate with another
6	virus	f	a unit of measurement for storing information
7	RAM	g	you can use it to transfer pictures to your computer
8	hardware	h	a program that destroys data and damages computers
9	hard disk	i	a series of linked electronic addresses all round the world
10	megabyte	j	a program for doing mathematical calculations
11	the Web	k	the place in your computer where information is stored

49.3 Choose the correct answer, (a), (b) or (c).

10 marks

1 Some people spend hours (a) serving (b) serfing (c) surfing the Web.
2 I can (a) e-post (b) e-mail (c) e-letter you tomorrow and send you the information.
3 I managed to (a) download (b) downput (c) downtake an interesting program from the Internet the other day.
4 Have you ever seen Madonna's (a) own page (b) home page (c) net page ?
5 My friend spends hours in those (a) speak (b) chat (c) talk rooms on the Internet.

49.4 Answer these questions.

10 marks

1 What does FAQ mean?
2 What do newsgroups do?
3 What is the short form of the word *Internet*?
4 Can you use your computer if it is 'down'?
5 Is an 'attachment' something you can receive with an e-mail? Yes or no.
6 What do you do to your mouse? You c.............. it.
7 If a program 'crashes', does it mean (a) you can't use it, or (b) it opens automatically?
8 What do the initials WWW mean?
9 What does the 'e' in 'e-mail' mean?
10 What is another name for a 'chat room'? A chat f.............. .

Your score

/40

TEST
50 The press and the media

50.1

10 marks

Explain the difference between:

Example: a series and a serial   Both are stories about the same characters; in a series, each episode contains a complete story whereas in a serial the plot continues from one episode to the next.

1 a tabloid and a quality newspaper
2 a journal and a magazine
3 making a film in a studio and making a film on location

4 an aerial and a satellite dish
5 sub-titling and dubbing

50.2

10 marks

Match the programme name (a–k) to its most likely programme type (1–11).

1 chat show
2 current affairs programme
3 detective story
4 documentary
5 game show
6 music programme
7 quiz
8 soap opera
9 sports programme
10 variety show
11 weather forecast

a Inspector Jack Investigates
b Win a Car
c Tomorrow's Weather
d Brain of Britain
e Dallas's Dynasty
f The World This Week
g Talking to Oprah
h Match of the Week
i The Secret Life of Turtles
j This Week's Top CDs
k Saturday Night at the Music Hall

50.3

10 marks

Each of these people can be found in either a newspaper office or a film studio. Where is each person most likely to be found?

Example: actor – film studio

~~actor~~	camera operator	cartoonist	censor	columnist	continuity person
critic	editor	foreign correspondent	make-up artist	sub-editor	

50.4

10 marks

Choose the right verb from the box and put it in the right form to complete the sentences.

broadcast	~~change~~	come out	cut	edit	lay out
pick up	print	publish	shoot	show	

Example: A remote control allows you to ...change........... channels from your sofa.

1 This book .... by Cambridge University Press.
2 The film .... on location in Siberia.
3 Can you .... Radio Tirana on your radio?
4 They .... *The Titanic* on TV again tonight.
5 Sunday newspapers .... once a week.
6 Censors sometimes order films ....
7 Some very good news programmes .... on the radio.
8 It is a sub-editor's job .... the pages of a newspaper.
9 Sub-editors are also often required .... articles which are too long.
10 Many British books .... in Hong Kong.

Your score

/40

TEST
51 Politics and public institutions

51.1

10 marks

Make a word that fits in the sentence and is based on the same root as the word in brackets.

Example: The political system in the UK is said to be ...democratic... . (democracy)

1 India gained its .... from Britain in 1947. (depend)
2 People vote for their representatives in an .... (elect)
3 I'd hate to live in a .... (dictate)
4 Some people feel the British .... will soon be abolished. (monarch)
5 An MP is the .... of his or her constituency. (represent)
6 The US has a system of presidential .... (govern)
7 In the UK the system is .... (parliament)
8 .... are elected for a fixed term. (senate)
9 Would you like to be a ....? (politics)
10 The Prime Minister selects his top .... (office)

51.2

10 marks

Divide the words into those used about the UK and those used about the US.

Example: Congress – US

~~Congress~~	House of Commons	House of Lords	House of Representatives
Monarch	MP	President	Prime Minister	Representative	Senate
Supreme Court			

51.3

10 marks

What word is being defined? The first letter is given.

Example: Government of, for and by the people. ...democracy...

1 One person whose word is law in a country. d.....................
2 A group of states with both local and central government. f.....................
3 The body which sees that laws are adhered to. j.....................
4 The body in a country that makes the laws. l.....................
5 A direct vote by the people on a public issue. r.....................

51.4

10 marks

Fill in the gaps with words from the box.

Example: One word meaning the king or queen of a country is the ...monarch... .

marginal	~~monarch~~	general	majority	by(e)-election
chambers	votes	overrule	ballot	candidates	policy

1 In a .... election, every constituency chooses an MP but in a .... only one MP is being elected.
2 The party which gets most votes is called the .... party.
3 If an MP only just wins his or her seat it is called a .... seat.
4 In many systems of government there are two ....; the USA has both the Senate and the House of Representatives, for example.
5 Voters cast their .... by marking a cross on their .... paper.
6 Voters choose from a list of ....
7 The government has to decide the country's economic ....
8 Although the judiciary is independent, it can't .... the Prime Minister's decisions.

Your score

/40

TEST
52 Crime

52.1

10 marks

What crimes are being defined below?

Example: offering someone money for illegal services   **bribery**

1 killing someone
2 stealing from a shop
3 selling drugs
4 making fake money
5 taking a child and asking
   its parents for money

6 driving after taking alcohol
7 stealing from people's pockets
8 threatening to reveal secrets
9 taking illegal control of a plane
10 taking something illegally into
    another country

52.2

10 marks

Complete the table.

crime	criminal	verb
forgery	*forger*	*forge*
murder		
		burgle
blackmail		
	kidnapper	
		rape

52.3

6 marks

Here are some words for things that may happen to criminals at the end of or after a trial. Put the letters in the right order to make the answers.

Example: TOCUYMIMN CVRSEEI   **community service**

1 NEFI
2 SIRPNO

3 BANTROPIO
4 OUISPOERCTN

5 TAHED NTYPEAL
6 ATCAUIQTL

52.4

14 marks

Use the words in the box to complete the paragraph. You must change the form of the verbs when necessary.

arrest	charge	~~commit~~	evidence	plead	prison	release
rob	sentence	serve	steal	time	trial	verdict	witness

Jake **committed** a crime when he (1)........................ a post office. He (2)........................ £5,000. A (3)........................ managed to take a photograph of him. The police (4)........................ him and (5)........................ him with robbery. The case came to court two months later. At his (6)........................ Jake (7)........................ not guilty. However, the photograph was used in (8)........................ against him and, as a result, the jury passed a (9)........................ of guilty. The judge (10)........................ him to ten years in (11)........................ . He (12)........................ eight years but then he (13)........................ having got (14)........................ off for good behaviour.

Your score
/40

TEST
53 Money – buying, selling and paying

53.1

10 marks

Use words from the box to complete the dialogue.

| charges | ~~current~~ | deposit | earn | instalments | loan |
| mortgage | overdrawn | pay | statement | withdraw |

CHILD: What do you use the bank for?
MUM: Well, we have a ...**current**... account where we pay in any money we
      (1)........................ . Then we can (2)........................ money from the account when we need to
      (3)........................ bills.
CHILD: How do you know how much money you've got?
MUM: They send us a (4)........................ every month telling us how much.
CHILD: What if you spend more than you've got?
MUM: Then you're (5)........................ and the bank usually (6)........................ you interest.
CHILD: What else do banks do?
MUM: Well, you can get a bank (7)........................ if you need to borrow a large sum of money.
CHILD: To buy a house, for example?
MUM: That's right. That's usually called a (8)........................ . It means the bank actually owns the
      house until you've paid the money back.
CHILD: How do you pay the money back?
MUM: You pay a (9)........................ first and then you pay monthly (10)........................ .

53.2

10 marks

What is the difference between ...?

Example: a current account and a savings account   *A current account is one you use
regularly for paying bills and a savings account is one where you leave any
extra money you have for a longer time so that you can get more interest.*

1 purchasing and haggling   3 a share and a dividend   5 a bargain and a rip-off
2 a profit and a loss   4 a discount and a refund

53.3

10 marks

What words are needed to complete the sentences?

Example: Sometimes students get a special ..**discount**.. on things they buy.

1 When you travel by bus you have to pay your ....
2 When you use a lawyer you have to pay a ....
3 When someone dies, their heir has to pay ....
4 On any money that you earn you have to pay ....
5 If you have paid too much tax, you should get a ....
6 VAT stands for ....
7 Large companies pay ....
8 If you import something you may be liable for ....
9 When you are old the government should pay you a ....
10 If you are out of work you may be able to claim ....

53.4

10 marks

Write a definition for each of these words or expressions.

1 buy in bulk   6 in the red
2 buy on credit   7 investment
3 cash   8 rate of exchange
4 credit card   9 salary
5 currency   10 wage

Your score

/ 40

TEST
54 Belief and opinion

54.1 Match the phrases on the left with the most suitable paraphrase on the right.

10 marks

1 I'm convinced that …	a I have an instinctive feeling …
2 I maintain that …	b I have some worries about …
3 I sense that …	c I guess or estimate that …
4 I have my doubts about …	d I do not think it is true …
5 I've always held that …	e I believe most strongly …
6 I reckon …	f I strongly support …
7 I'm in favour of …	g I am opposed to …
8 I feel …	h I believe it, even if it seems doubtful …
9 I doubt that …	i I have consistently believed that …
10 I suspect that …	j I have a negative feeling about something …
11 I'm against …	k I have a strong personal opinion that …

54.2 Fill the gaps.

10 marks

1 In my .... / .... , the whole system should be changed (*two possibilities: 2 marks*)
2 They've put it in the wrong place, to my ....
3 If you .... me, she ought to give up her studies and get a job.
4 .... the patients' point of view, the new hospital is a long way from anywhere.
5 Do you believe .... ghosts? I think I saw one once in an old house.
6 What do you think .... my new computer? Smart, isn't it?
7 What are your views .... genetically modified food?
8 Are you .... or .... keeping the Antarctic as a protected zone? (*2 marks*)

54.3 Find five more pairs of synonyms in the box.

10 marks

fanatical	traditional	middle-of-the-road	firm	obsessive	dedicated
odd	conservative	eccentric	moderate	strong	committed

54.4 What do we call …

10 marks

1 a person who follows the philosophy of Charles Darwin.
2 a person who belongs to the religion based on the teaching of the prophet Mohammed.
3 a person who believes in socialism.
4 a person who does not eat meat.
5 a person who refuses to fight in a war and who believes in non-violence.
6 a person who always wants to do everything absolutely perfectly.
7 a person who always takes the traditional line in everything.

What adjective means …? The first letters are given.

8 open to new ideas and willing to be persuaded. o...............-m...............
9 having very original and strong thoughts (e.g. about politics). r...............
10 having beliefs which cannot be shaken and who refuses to compromise. d...............

Your score

/40

TEST
55 Pleasant and unpleasant feelings

55.1

10 marks

Do these adjectives describe pleasant or unpleasant feelings? Divide them into two groups.

Example: happy   pleasant

anxious	apprehensive	cheerful	contented	cross	delighted	depressed
ecstatic	excited	fed-up	frustrated	grateful	~~happy~~	livid	miserable
mixed-up	nervous	seething	thrilled	upset	worried	

55.2

10 marks

What are the nouns relating to each of these adjectives?

Example: happy   happiness

1 anxious	3 cheerful	5 contented	7 delighted	9 depressed
2 enthusiastic	4 excited	6 frustrated	8 grateful	10 inspired

55.3

10 marks

You need an adjective ending in either *-ed* or *-ing* to complete each sentence. Use the word in brackets to form the adjective you need.

Example: Rob's mother was ..horrified.......... by his news. (horrify)

1 Meena was .... to get such a good job. (thrill)
2 I find the figures very .... Could you explain them, please? (confuse)
3 Leo Cone's songs can be terribly .... (depress)
4 Rab's been feeling .... in his work for some time now. (frustrate)
5 Poets often find nature .... (inspire)
6 This report is very .... (worry)
7 We are very .... about our holiday plans. (excite)
8 Jo seems rather .... Do you know what the matter is? (depress)
9 Rick told me some .... news last night. (thrill)
10 I'm rather .... about Jim at the moment. (worry)

55.4

10 marks

Choose the adjective from the box below which best describes how the speaker is feeling in each case.

Example: I just don't know what to think. One moment everything seems fine, the next it's all at sixes and sevens again.   confused

boiling	~~confused~~	contented	excited	freezing	furious
grateful	inspired	nervous	starving	worn out	

1 Thank you so much. I could never have managed without your help!
2 I wish I hadn't got to go to the dentist tomorrow. I hate having teeth filled.
3 Look at that wonderful rainbow! I must write a poem.
4 I'm so hungry I could eat a horse.
5 It's very hot in the sun. Let's go into the shade.
6 He should never have behaved like that towards you. It's disgraceful!
7 I'm desperately tired after digging the garden all day.
8 It should be a brilliant party. I'm really looking forward to it!
9 I love my little flat. I never want to live anywhere else now.
10 It's terribly cold in here. I need a thick jumper – or two!

Your score

/40

TEST
56 Like, dislike and desire

56.1

10 marks

Reword the sentences without changing the meaning. Use the word in brackets.

Example: Jo very much wants to be with her family again. (to yearn) *Jo yearns to be with her family again.*

1 I strongly disapprove of his behaviour. (to appal)
2 It's been so difficult at work – I can't wait for my holiday. (to long)
3 Maria likes romantic novels very much. (fond)
4 Amy didn't fancy Bob. (attractive)
5 He loves his daughter more than anyone else in the world. (to care)
6 Sam worshipped his wife. (devoted)
7 I detest standing in queues. (to bear)
8 Did you have a good time at the party? (to enjoy)
9 I loathe violence on TV. (to disgust)
10 I always hate the thought of going back to work after a holiday. (to dread)

56.2

10 marks

Insert the correct prepositions in the paragraph below.

Sally fell ..*in*.... love (1).............. Tom the moment she first set eyes (2).............. him. She was captivated (3).............. his beautiful smile and his kindness (4).............. everyone he cared (5).............. . She had been looking (6).............. to going (7).............. holiday but, once she had met him, she was no longer keen (8).............. the idea of going away in case he decided to invite her (9).............. . Fortunately, Tom had also fallen (10).............. Sally.

56.3

10 marks

Complete the following table.

verb	noun	adjective
attract	*attraction*	*attractive*
appeal		
tempt		
repel		
revolt		
disgust		
adore		
desire		
enjoy		
fascinate		
hate		

56.4

10 marks

Are the following statements true or false? When false, correct them.

Example: Kleptomaniacs are constantly tempted to break things. *False. Kleptomaniacs are constantly tempted to steal things.*

1 Claustrophobics can't stand Father Christmas.
2 Marxists are passionate about Groucho Marx.
3 Sadists enjoy feeling depressed.
4 Ornithologists are fascinated by horns.
5 Misogynists loathe unmarried women.

Your score

/40

TEST
57 Speaking

57.1
10 marks
Complete the statements with the most appropriate verb. Put the verb into the correct form.

beg	boast	complain	confess	grumble	murmur
insist	~~scream~~	stutter	threaten	urge	

Example: 'There's a mouse. I can't stand mice,' she <u>screamed</u> .

1 'I'll contact my lawyer if you lay a finger on my daughter,' he ....
2 'I c-c-c-can't h-h-help you,' .... Bob.
3 'I'm far better than the other students in my class,' Gill ....
4 'You really must be here by 8,' .... the teacher.
5 'I read your diary,' he ....
6 'You're the most beautiful girl in the world,' he .... in her ear.
7 'My glass is dirty,' she ....
8 'Please, please, lend me the money.' he ....
9 'I don't want to do my homework,' .... the child.
10 'Just have one more try. You're nearly there,' .... his mother.

57.2
10 marks
The verbs in the previous sentences could be replaced with 'said + an adverb'. Use *said* + the most appropriate adverb from the box below to replace the verbs in exercise 1. Make any necessary changes to word order.

angrily	crossly	desperately	encouragingly	~~fearfully~~	firmly
furiously	guiltily	nervously	proudly	softly	

Example: 'There's a mouse. I can't stand mice,' she <u>said fearfully</u> .

57.3
12 marks
Fill the gaps with a preposition and the appropriate form of the verb in brackets.

Example: Will Sue ever stop boasting <u>about winning</u> first prize? (win)

1 The girl's father insisted .... her .... home before midnight. (get)
2 I really object .... people .... in my house. (smoke)
3 They are always grumbling .... to work on Sundays. (have)
4 The accused has never confessed .... the murder. (commit)
5 He begged me .... money and then begged me .... him find somewhere to live. (help)
6 John complained .... his boss about his colleague .... sacked. (be)

57.4
8 marks
Pair the verbs on the left with the verbs that are very close in meaning on the right.

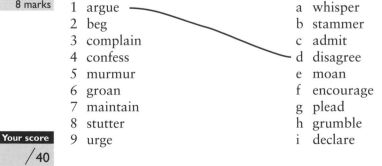

1 argue   a whisper
2 beg   b stammer
3 complain   c admit
4 confess   d disagree
5 murmur   e moan
6 groan   f encourage
7 maintain   g plead
8 stutter   h grumble
9 urge   i declare

Your score
/40

TEST
58 The six senses

58.1
10 marks

People have five physical senses – sight, hearing, taste, touch and smell. Which of those senses do each of these verbs or adjectives go with?

Example: aromatic   smell

~~aromatic~~	bitter	deafen	glimpse	grasp
peer	pungent	quiet	spicy	stink	tap

58.2
10 marks

Use all the words in the boxes to make ten statements.

Example: Alice has won a holiday in Bali. She feels very excited.

1 Alice has won a holiday in Bali. She		very pleasant.
2 Anna is going on a diet. She's slim but she says she		too sweet.
3 Do you think he's going to be sick? He		so soft.
4 Have you heard about their trip to Nepal? It	feels	very exciting.
5 Here comes the bride! She	looks	fat.
6 I haven't met Jill's new teacher yet but she	smells	a bit tasteless.
7 I love stroking the cat. It	sounds	so fragrant.
8 I love this rose. It	tastes	wonderful.
9 No one has lived in this house for ages. It		rather green.
10 They've put too much chocolate in this cake. It		musty.
11 This soup needs more salt and pepper. It		very excited.

58.3
5 marks

Match the phenomena on the left with an example of it on the right.

1 déjà vu	a experiencing any of the phenomena in this exercise
2 intuition	b dreaming about an accident before it occurs
3 premonition	c thinking about a friend a second before she rings you
4 sixth sense	d walking into a place and feeling you've been there before
5 telepathy	e sensing why a close friend is upset

58.4
15 marks

Fill the gaps by choosing the best verb. Put the verb in the correct form.

Example: The old lady sat ̲s̲t̲r̲o̲k̲i̲n̲g̲. her cat. (handle/stroke/knock/tap)

1 I .... a terrible accident on my way to work. (glance/peer/stare/witness)
2 The old man .... the little boy on his head. (grab/grasp/pat/handle)
3 Every few minutes the girl .... at her watch. (glance/glimpse/observe/witness)
4 You'll have to .... on the door as the bell doesn't work. (finger/knock/pat/stroke)
5 Please .... the ornaments carefully when dusting them. (finger/grasp/handle/press)
6 When you finish your phone call, be sure .... the red button. (grab/knock/pat/press)
7 She .... at the map as if she needed new glasses. (gaze/notice/observe/peer)
8 They .... lovingly into each other's eyes. (gaze/glimpse/observe/see)
9 The child .... the last cake and ran out of the room. (grasp/knock/snatch/stroke)
10 The police .... the suspect's house. (notice/observe/stare/witness)

Your score
/40

TEST
59 What your body does

59.1
10 marks

Match the word on the left with its definition on the right.

1	bite	a	smile broadly
2	blink	b	noise a hungry stomach makes
3	blush	c	perspire
4	breathe	d	cut through something with your teeth
5	grin	e	deep breath taken when relieved or unhappy
6	rumble	f	heavy breathing noise made when asleep
7	shiver	g	use your lungs to take in air and to exhale
8	sigh	h	open and close both eyes rapidly
9	snore	i	close one eye
10	sweat	j	tremble with cold
11	wink	k	go red

59.2
10 marks

These mixed-up words all describe things that parts of your body can do. What are these things? Put the letters in the right order and explain what the words mean.

Example: K N W I wink – close one eye

1 K E H A S   6 U G O C H
2 K I L C   7 W A N Y
3 P U R B   8 E T R E B A H
4 W H E C   9 C I C H O G H U
5 E N S Z E E   10 L R E E B T M

59.3
10 marks

These sentences have been mixed up. Move the parts in italics to where they make sense.

Example: Suck this sweet to stop your ears popping as the plane descends.

1 ~~Suck this sweet~~ *because her children are behaving so badly.*
2 Drink this water *because his hands are trembling.*
3 Having had so little sleep last night, *you digest it more easily.*
4 Hold your breath for 30 seconds *to see if you can get the dust out of your eye.*
5 If you chew your food well, *he's been yawning all day.*
6 She's frowning *and you should stop hiccoughing.*
7 Some people sneeze *to help you swallow the pill.*
8 She sighed with relief *if they come into contact with a cat.*
9 Try blinking *whenever she's embarrassed.*
10 You can tell that he's nervous *when she heard Nick had arrived safely.*
11 She always blushes ~~*to stop your ears popping as the plane descends*~~.

59.4
10 marks

Which is the odd one out? Explain why.

Example: cough, (frown), sigh, yawn All the others are connected with breathing in some way, whereas frown is a kind of facial expression.

1 shake, shiver, sigh, tremble
2 chew, lick, rumble, suck
3 blink, blush, wink, frown
4 burp, hiccough, snore, cough
5 cough, grin, shiver, sneeze

Your score
/ 40

60 Number, quantity, degree and intensity

60.1

10 marks

Divide these words into two groups: 'small' words and 'big' words.

~~gigantic~~   vast   minuscule   minute   huge   tiny
enormous   meagre   sizeable   insignificant   considerable

small	
big	*gigantic*

60.2

5 marks

Fill the gaps with a suitable word. The first letter is given.

1 Even a t.............. amount of dust can damage a computer disk.
2 She's had a h.............. amount of work lately. She looks so tired.
3 There was t.............. of food at the party. I'm sorry I had dinner before I went there.
4 It takes a c.............. amount of money to set up your own company.
5 An e.............. amount of fat in his diet put him at risk from a heart attack.

60.3

5 marks

Fill the gaps with one of the expressions in the box. Use each expression once only.

a good deal of   heaps of   a small amount of   much   a very small number of

1 Do you have .... work to do? Shall I help?
2 Only .... students failed the exams, so the headteacher was very pleased.
3 We don't need to hurry. There's .... time. The train doesn't leave till six.
4 The government has put .... effort into reducing unemployment.
5 There was .... oil on the surface which we had to clean off. It wasn't serious.

60.4

14 marks

Put ticks (✓) in the boxes where the words normally collocate. For example, we can say *totally/utterly destroyed*, but not normally *rather/a bit destroyed*.

	a bit	totally	rather	utterly
cool (temperature)				
destroyed		✓		✓
ridiculous				
worried				
wrong				
big				
ruined				

60.5

6 marks

What word or expression is ...

1 connected with the number twelve, and means 'a lot of'?
2 used for just a small amount of liquid?
3 a name for a measurement of weight, and means 'a lot of'?
4 based on the word *bag*, and means 'a lot of'?
5 used to mean 'a typical number, no more or less than usual'?
6 like the word for 'sixty seconds', but means 'small', and has a different pronunciation?

TEST
61 Time

61.1
10 marks

Fill the gaps with a suitable time word beginning with the letter given.

Example: During the Stone A.............. , humans developed new tools and instruments.

1 We had a very hot s.............. of weather in April and no rain at all.
2 When the war ended, a new e.............. of peace and prosperity began.
3 We lived in New York for a t.............. when I was a child.
4 For a p.............. of six months, I had no contact with her whatsoever.
5 Why don't you go and have a lie-down for a w.............. .

61.2
12 marks

Choose one of the phrases to fill the gap.

for the time being	at times	by the time	one at a time
~~just in time~~	on time	time and time again	

Example: I got to the airport *just in time* to say goodbye to her.

1 I warned you .... to make copies of everything in case the computer crashed.
2 Everybody arrived .... , so we were able to start at exactly nine o'clock.
3 The new computer is arriving next week. Can you use the old one .... ?
4 The teacher saw the students .... to tell each one their exam results privately.
5 I get very lonely ....
6 The traffic was terrible. .... I got to the station, the train had gone.

61.3
10 marks

Say whether these statements are True or False.

		True	*False*
1	'Ten years have elapsed' is more formal than 'ten years have passed'.	☐	☐
2	'It lasts ten hours to fly from London to Singapore' is correct English.	☐	☐
3	The verb *elapse* is used with a wide range of tenses.		
4	'The batteries in my personal stereo last about ten hours' is correct English.	☐	☐
5	We can say 'This video tape will run for three hours'.	☐	☐
6	'The meeting went on for three hours' means 'I was actually expecting it to last for five hours'.	☐	☐
7	'Take your time!' means 'Hurry up!'	☐	☐
8	The verb *pass* is used with a wide range of tenses to talk about time.	☐	☐
9	'Time elapsed quickly' is correct English.	☐	☐
10	'Time passed slowly' is correct English.	☐	☐

61.4
8 marks

Rewrite the sentences using these words.

temporary	permanent	provisional	~~timeless~~	eternal

Example: The city of Rome has a beauty that will never change. **The city of Rome has a timeless beauty.**

1 The job was just for three months, replacing someone who was sick.
2 Many people believe in a life after death which never ends.
3 After a year, the job became one she could keep all her life.
4 We reached an agreement which was not absolutely definite.

Your score

/40

TEST 62 Distances and dimensions

62.1 Put a tick (✓) in the box if the statement is correct. Put a cross (✗) if it is wrong.

12 marks

1 A *wide road* is a more commonly used phrase than *a broad road*. ☐
2 We can say *a tall building* and *a tall person*. ☐
3 We can say *a high person*. ☐
4 *Broad* is often used with abstract words such as *range*, *subject*. ☐
5 *Long* comes before a measurement, e.g. *The room is long 4.5 metres*. ☐
6 *Shallow* means 'not very long'. ☐

62.2 Fill in the missing words.

8 marks

noun	verb	adjective
depth		deep
		long
width		
		short
breadth		broad
height		

62.3 Use forms of the words *long, short, wide, high, broad, low, far* and *deep* to fill the gaps.

10 marks

Example: The ..length.. of the new swimming pool is 25 metres.

1 The authorities have decided to .... the road to allow more traffic to use it.
2 Is there a ....-............... to the town centre? I'm in a hurry.
3 She .... her trousers because she thought they were too short.
4 The darkness .... our feeling of loneliness out there on the sea.
5 He always loves to go to .... places for his holidays.
6 Could you .... the sleeves for me? They are much too long.
7 The decision of the government .... the crisis and war was inevitable.
8 Travel is good for you; it .... your mind.
9 Getting a visa is a .... process; it can take up to two months.
10 Could you .... the mirror please; it's too high for me.

62.4 Rewrite the sentences using the correct form of the words given.

10 marks

Example: The company's activities have become smaller in recent years. (contract)
   The company's activities have contracted in recent years.

1 There was very rapid growth in the economy last year. (expand)
2 We are going to build onto our house. (extend)
3 This shirt got smaller when I washed it. (shrink)
4 The city has got bigger in the last ten years. (grow)
5 New houses have been built in the countryside. (spread)

Your score
/40

TEST

63 Obligation, need, possibility and probability

63.1

10 marks

Fill the gaps with words connected with obligation beginning with the letter given.

1 English is a c........................ subject in all secondary schools.
2 The concert was cancelled; the organisers were o........................ to give us our money back.
3 A life sentence is m........................ for anyone who commits murder.
4 No, you do not have to do it, it's o........................ .
5 Most students are e........................ from paying tax.
6 We had no a........................ but to sell our house.
7 The terrorists f........................ their victims to lie on the floor with their eyes closed.
8 You are l........................ for damage to a rented car, unless you take out extra insurance.
9 You must take the exam. You have no c........................ .
10 Military service is o........................ in many countries for everyone over the age of 18.

63.2

10 marks

Rewrite the sentences using the words in brackets.

Example: Water is a basic thing that human life must have. (necessity)
Water is a basic necessity for human life.

1 There were not enough engineers so a foreign company built the road. (shortage)
2 The astronauts died because they did not have enough oxygen. (lack of)
3 When I got home after being away, all my plants needed water. (in need)
4 More discussion is needed before we can make a decision. (need for)
5 The garden needs to be watered before we put the new flowers in. (want)

63.3

6 marks

Arrange these words on a scale from 'cannot be or will not be' to 'must be'.

certain	possible	unlikely	inevitable	impossible	probable

CANNOT BE
TRUE ⟵|————|————|————|————|————|⟶ MUST BE
      1   2   3   4   5   6   TRUE

63.4

4 marks

Fill the gaps with *must, have (got) to, possibility* or *opportunity*.

1 I've been given the .... to go to the USA with my basketball team. Isn't it great?
2 Because I don't have a car any more, I .... take the bus every day now.
3 I really .... ring Mr Sullivan. I promised him I would do it last week, then forgot.
4 Is there any .... of changing the date of the meeting?

63.5

10 marks

Collocation test. Put a tick (✓) if the collocation is typical, put a cross (✗) if it is not typical.

	highly	quite	very	absolutely
possible	✗	✓	✓	✗
impossible				
probable				
(un)likely				
inevitable				
certain				

Your score

/40

TEST
64 Sound and light

64.1 **Choose the correct answer, (a) or (b).**

10 marks

1 I could hear the <u>noise/sound</u> of a gentle stream running just outside the house.
2 The neighbours made a lot of <u>noises/noise</u> last night at their party.
3 The children are making a terrible <u>racket/sound.</u> Go and tell them to be quiet.
4 The room was rather <u>dim/sombre</u> so we painted it white and got some colourful curtains.
5 The light from the lamp was rather <u>noisy/dim</u>, so we got a stronger one.
6 It was a beautiful night, with thousands of stars <u>flashing/twinkling</u> in the sky.
7 The car's headlights gave out a strong <u>twinkle/beam</u> of light which shone across the river.
8 A camera <u>flashed/flickered</u> and we knew someone had taken a photograph of us.
9 The sky is looking very <u>gloomy/flashing</u>; I think it's going to snow.
10 I heard some strange <u>rackets/noises</u> last night. I wonder what it was?

64.2 **Match the words on the left with something on the right that makes the sound. Draw lines as in the example.**

20 marks

1	roar	a	piles of dry leaves blown by the wind
2	clatter	b	thunder in the distance
3	thud	c	gas escaping from a pipe
4	pop	d	rain falling on a metal roof
5	bang	e	someone hitting a big metal bell
6	crash	f	a jumbo jet taking off
7	hiss	g	a cork coming out of a bottle
8	rustle	h	pots and pans being moved in a kitchen
9	clang	i	a balloon as it bursts
10	rumble	j	a heavy object falling on to a carpeted floor
11	patter	k	a big, heavy object falling on to a stone floor

64.3 **Fill the gaps. You are given the first and last letters of the missing word.**

10 marks

1 The sun was s..............ing and beautiful r..............s of light were coming in through my window.
2 The exhibition of ancient treasure was wonderful, with jewels s..............ing and gold objects g..............ing all round us.
3 The candle f..............d in the breeze and then went out.
4 We could hear thousands of insects buzzing and h..............ing in the bushes.
5 She r..............d her tin of money and asked us to give something to help the Children's Hospital.
6 My mobile phone b..............s to warn me when the battery is low.
7 The tyres s..............d as the bank robbers drove off at high speed.
8 We could hear bells c..............ing in the distance. Perhaps it was a wedding.

Your score

/40

TEST
65 Possession, giving and lending

65.1

10 marks

Match the words on the left with their definitions on the right.

1 estate   a small items you carry with you (e.g. your bag, coat, wallet, camera)
2 wealth   b a person who pays rent to live in a house or flat
3 a property   c all the things and money you leave after your death
4 belongings   d everything you own
5 a tenant   e a house and the land it is on
6 possessions   f having a lot of money

65.2

5 marks

Answer the questions.

1 What do we call the person you pay rent to if you live in their house or flat?
2 What is a rather formal word for the person who owns a shop or restaurant?
3 What is a general word for anyone who owns something (e.g. a house, a bicycle, land)?
4 What is the noun form of the verb *to lend*?
5 What verb beginning with *d-* can we use to mean 'to give something (often a large sum of money or some valuable items) to an institution'?

65.3

5 marks

Fill the gaps using the words in the box. In one case, two words are possible; give yourself 2 marks for this one.

| hire | rent | lend | borrow |

1 Can you .... me ten pounds? I'll give it back to you tomorrow.
2 He asked if he could .... my camera for a couple of days.
3 It would be fun to .... a car and have a holiday in the north of the country.
4 How expensive is it to .... a flat near the university?

65.4

10 marks

Rewrite the sentences using the verbs given. Marks for each sentence are given separately.

1 Would you like to help the Children's Hospital? (contribute) (*1 mark*)
2 This river is where the people of the village get their water. (provide) (*2 marks*)
3 Which company sells you paper and envelopes? (supply) (*1 mark*)
4 I'd like to give you this cheque for £300 from all of us here. (present) (*2 marks*)
5 When my grandfather died, there was £2000 for the local hospital. (leave) (*1 mark*)
6 The company restaurant looks after 300 people every day. (cater) (*2 marks*)
7 All the best jobs had already been given out, so there were only unpleasant jobs left. (allocate) (*1 mark*)

65.5

10 marks

Use the words in the box to fill the gaps to complete these phrasal verbs.

| of | out | down | up | over | away |

1 The teacher gave .... the exam papers five minutes before the exam began.
2 I haven't got a baseball bat any more; I gave it ....
3 She asked if I would sell that old 1955 car I've got, but I don't want to let go .... it.
4 The mugger made her hand .... her cash and credit cards.
5 This picture has been handed .... in my family for generations.

Your score

/ 40

TEST
66 Movement and speed

66.1 Connect the words in the left-hand column with an appropriate verb in the middle column
and an appropriate sentence-ending in the right-hand column.

10 marks

1	The car	stirred	across the sky.
2	The river	swayed	directly over our house.
3	The ferry	drifted	slowly along the busy motorway.
4	The traffic	fluttered	away at high speed with four people in it.
5	The train	travelled	in the breeze.
6	The clouds	drove	to avoid a cat.
7	The flag	moved	across the channel.
8	The leaves	flowed	in the gentle breeze.
9	The trees	flew	at high speed along the new track.
10	The lorry	sailed	through the valley.
11	The plane	swerved	in the strong wind.

66.2 Put these words into two categories: 'slow' words and 'fast' words. Put S for slow and F for
fast.

8 marks

dawdle ☐   hurry ☐   tear ☐   creep ☐

trundle ☐   shoot ☐   plod ☐   rush ☐

66.3 Use these words to fill the gaps.

8 marks

speed	rate	pace	velocity

1 This gun fires a high-.............. bullet which can penetrate metal.
2 The birth-.............. in Europe has decreased in the last thirty years.
3 Japan has some of the best high-.............. trains in the world.
4 The lesson went at a very slow .... and the students got bored.

66.4 Answer the questions.

14 marks

1 What sort of child is a *toddler*?
2 What sort of person is a *slowcoach*?
3 What type of person is a *plodder*?
4 If someone was called a *drifter*, what sort of person are they?
5 Is *fast* an adjective, an adverb or both?
6 Are *rapid* and *swift* similar in meaning or opposite in meaning?
7 Which is the more typical collocation, *a fast car* or *a quick car*?

Your score
/40

TEST
67 Texture, brightness, weight and density

67.1 Match the words on the left with a suitable object on the right.

10 marks

1	rough	a	a floor that is highly polished and wet in places
2	smooth	b	large grains of sand
3	polished	c	very, very thin paper or a dried leaf
4	coarse	d	a cactus
5	sleek	e	broken glass
6	gnarled	f	a cement or concrete surface
7	delicate	g	a baby's skin
8	slippery	h	a teddy bear
9	furry	i	the exterior of a brand-new sports car
10	jagged	j	an old, dead tree trunk
11	prickly	k	a mirror

67.2 Fill the gaps. The first and last letters are given.

10 marks

1 The new-born baby's hair was soft and d..............y.
2 This paper is very smooth to the t..............h.
3 The fields were very wet u..............t after the heavy rain.
4 This blouse feels very s..............y, but in fact it's not real silk.
5 The s..............e of the table was highly polished.

67.3 Say whether these statements are true (T) or false (F).

10 marks

1 *Shady* is the adjective related to the noun *shade*. ☐
2 If a light is *dazzling* is is not very bright. ☐
3 *Vivid colours* and *dull colours* mean the same. ☐
4 A *dim* light is the opposite of a *bright* light. ☐
3 People often wear sunglasses to protect their eyes against the glare ☐
   of the sun.

67.4 Answer the questions. You are sometimes given the first letter of the answer.

10 marks

1 What adjective could you use to describe a tree that has no solid interior? h..............
2 What adjective could be used to describe the opposite of *thick* hair for a person? ....
3 What adjective could be used to describe very thick vegetation? d..............
4 What is the opposite of thick vegetation? s..............
5 Give another word for *heavy*, which can be used for things. w..............
6 Complete this phrase: *as light as a* ....
7 Give two words that mean 'heavy and awkward to move or carry'. b.............. and c..............
   (*2 marks*)
8 Complete this phrase: *as heavy as* ....
9 What adjective comes from the verb *shine*? ....

Your score

/40

TEST
68 Success, failure and difficulty

68.1 Correct the mistakes in these sentences. The part to correct is in bold.

10 marks

Example: We **managed finishing** the project a week in advance. ......*managed to finish*....

1 I **succeeded to persuade** him to come with us.
2 I'll jog with you, but I don't think I can **succeed ten kilometres**. Can we do five instead?
3 We have **accomplished to do** a great deal this year.
4 I'm not sure her plan will **come away**, but I hope it does, for her sake.
5 The company has not **achieved to reach** its targets for this year.

68.2 Put a tick (✓) if the word in the vertical column normally collocates with the word in the horizontal column. For example, one possible collocation for 'dream' is 'fulfil a dream'.

10 marks

You should end up with 10 ticks of your own.

	reach	attain	secure	realise	fulfil	achieve
an ambition						
a dream					✓	
an agreement						
an obligation						
a compromise						

68.3 Fill the gaps.

1 Our plans went w............... and we had to think again.
2 Their plans back............... and disaster resulted.

10 marks

3 The local nature society f............... after only six months through lack of members.
4 The project has f............... a couple of times, but I think it will succed in the long term.
5 The proposal to build a new town hall came to n............... in the end; most people were quite happy with the old one.
6 I f............... it difficult to read very small print. I need glasses.
7 I've had a lot of t............... with this camera; I'm very disappointed with it.
8 Can you c............... with my three sisters coming to stay? I hope it won't be too much work.
9 We've experienced some d............... in contacting her, but we'll keep trying.
10 The new exam system has caused a lot of b............... for everyone; I think we should have stuck with the old one.

68.4 Complete the table. Do not put anything in the shaded boxes. ▨

10 marks

noun	verb	adjective	adverb
	succeed		
	accomplish	*accomplished*	
attainment			
	achieve		
	fulfil		

Your score
/40

TEST
69 Idioms and fixed expressions – general

69.1

10 marks

Match the idioms on the left with a suitable sentence on the right. Draw lines as in the example.

1 Stop making a meal out of it.
2 We've got to make a move.
3 I think I'll hit the sack.
4 He's always on the make.
5 She really pulled a fast one.
6 Don't poke your nose in.
7 I'm over the moon.
8 I'm really down in the dumps today.
9 I'm in the red.
10 She's a pain in the neck.
11 He's as daft as a brush sometimes.

a We were tricked out of the money.
b He's just in it for his own personal profit.
c Just look at the clock.
d It's been such a depressing day.
e It was a small mistake – it's not important.
f She annoys so many people.
g It's been a long day and I'm exhausted.
h I'm absolutely delighted with the news.
i I thought I had more in my bank account.
j He found his keys in the fridge this morning.
k You shouldn't interfere in other people's business.

69.2

26 marks

Use the key words in the list to fill in gaps in the idioms

| weather | weight | biscuit | bark | stick | pie | days |
| ocean | clanger | plate | handle | chip | shot | |

1 I'm afraid she's got the wrong end of the .... Let me explain what actually happened. I hope you'll believe me, not her.
2 I dropped a .... when I said to Bill that American coffee was always too weak; I didn't realise he was American.
3 We don't really know what the answer is; this is just a .... in the dark.
4 I feel a bit under the .... today. I think I'll stay in bed. I'll be fine tomorrow.
5 He's ....ing up the wrong tree; it was last week it happened, not this week. He must be thinking of something else.
6 Come in, Bob. Here, have this armchair. Take the .... off your feet.
7 My old car's seen better .... It's time to buy a new one, I think.
8 When it comes to misunderstanding everything, Norman really takes the .... I've never met anyone quite like him.
9 I can't take on even more responsibility. I've enough on my .... as it is!
10 Politicians are always making promises, but they're usually just .... in the sky.
11 He just flew off the .... when I mentioned it. He has such a short temper!
12 100 pounds is just a drop in the .... compared with how much profit the bank makes every year.
13 Ted is a real .... off the old block; his father was just the same, totally lazy!

69.3

4 marks

Choose which grammatical form of the idiom is correct.

1 She **sits / is sitting** pretty with that new job of hers; she has a huge office, a big salary and a company car, and doesn't have much to do.
2 If you want a country with a combination of cultures, Malaysia **springs / is springing** to mind as a perfect example of different cultures living side by side.
3 He **was barking / barked** up the wrong tree when he said it was Jo's fault. Someone should tell him the truth.
4 Her attitude **is leaving / leaves** a lot to be desired. She should learn to treat people properly.

Your score

/ 40

TEST
70 Everyday expressions

70.1

10 marks

Match the sentences with a suitable definition of the idioms in bold.

Sentences

1 **As I was saying**, we'll need to get up early tomorrow.
2 **As you say**, it won't happen before July.
3 **Talking of** engineers, how's that cousin of yours who worked in Africa?
4 **If you ask me**, it's completely unnecessary.
5 **That reminds me**, I haven't rung George yet.
6 **Come to think of it**, George still hasn't got in touch. I wonder what's happening.
7 **If all else fails**, you can ring me on this number.
8 **If the worst comes to the worst**, we'll have to cancel the meeting.
9 **What with one thing and another**, I haven't had time to write my report.
10 **When it comes to** opera singers, Pamparoni is the best in the world, in my opinion.

Definitions

a something in the conversation makes you remember something important
b if you have tried everything but are not successful
c if the situation gets very bad and there is no alternative
d because of a lot of different circumstances
e starting a new topic but linking it to the present one
f if it is a question of/if we are talking about
g takes the conversation back to an earlier point
h something in the conversation makes you realise there may be a problem/query about something
i repeats and confirms something someone has already said
j if you want my opinion (even if no-one has asked for it)

70.2

12 marks

Complete the diagram by filling the gaps with *this* or *that*.

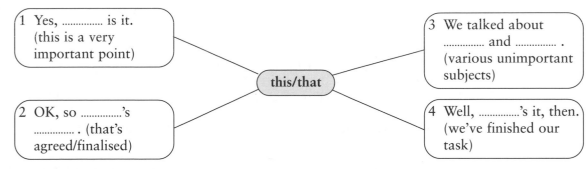

1 Yes, ... is it. (this is a very important point)

2 OK, so ....'s .... (that's agreed/finalised)

this/that

3 We talked about .... and .... (various unimportant subjects)

4 Well, ...'s it, then. (we've finished our task)

70.3

18 marks

Answer the questions.

1 What expression with *now* means 'right away, with no delay'?
2 What expression with *now* can be used to start a new, important topic in a discussion?
3 What expression with *now* means 'occasionally/from time to time'? Give two alternatives (*total 6 marks: 3 marks per expression*)
4 What expression means 'from my point of view' and includes the word 'far'?
5 What expression means 'by chance' and includes the word *luck*?

Your score
/ 40

TEST

71 Similes

71.1

10 marks

Complete the following similes with the words from the box.

~~blind~~	bold	bone	bull	deaf	drunk
fish	horse	iron	mad	ox	

Example: as ..blind.. as a bat

1 as .... as a lord
2 as .... as a hatter
3 as .... as a post
4 to eat like a ....
5 as hard as ....

6 as dry as a ....
7 as strong as an ....
8 to drink like a ....
9 as .... as brass
10 to behave like a .... in a china shop

71.2

10 marks

Agree with the following statements. Use a simile.

Example: Joanna's very tanned after her holiday. **Yes, she's as brown as a berry.**

1 The children behaved very well yesterday.

....

2 Jim never has too much to drink.

....

3 Didn't he blush when she smiled at him!

....

4 Bill never says a word, does he?

....

5 I couldn't believe how little she weighs.

....

71.3

10 marks

What do these sentences mean?

Example: The exam was as easy as falling off a log. **The exam was very easy.**

1 I slept like a log.
2 He was as sick as a dog all night.
3 The goalkeeper was as sick as a parrot after the match.
4 When she heard the news she went as white as a sheet.
5 The lady's hands were as white as snow.

71.4

10 marks

Reword these sentences using similes with *as* or *like* and the words in brackets. Use two similes in sentences 1, 3 and 6.

Example: I was terribly sick after eating so many sausages last night. **I was as sick as a dog after eating so many sausages last night.**

1 She's very thin but very strong. (rake; ox)
2 He's in a very bad temper today. (bear)
3 He's terribly forgetful and is completely mad. (head; hatter)
4 His grandmother notices everything that we do. (hawk)
5 She looked really cool even though it was 30° in the shade. (cucumber)
6 My plan worked really well and the work was done very quickly. (dream; flash)
7 Party political broadcasts on TV really make him mad. (bull)

Your score

/40

TEST

72 Binomials

72.1

10 marks

Binomials are fixed expressions where two words are joined by a conjunction, e.g. black and white, up and down. Connect words from box A with words from box B using *and* to make binomial expressions.

A	give	prim	rant	rough	wine	part	odds	rack	leaps	pick

B	parcel	rave	take	ruin	ready	proper	choose	bounds	dine	ends

72.2

10 marks

Now use the expressions from 72.1 above to fill the gaps.

1 The hotel was a bit .... and .... , but it was cheap and convenient.
2 The new boss is very .... and .... The old one was more informal and easy-going.
3 The secret of a successful marriage is .... and .... ; being ready to compromise.
4 He was furious and started to .... and .... at us.
5 My English has progressed in .... and .... during this course.
6 Hard work is .... and .... of learning a language; there's no other way.
7 My friends in New York always .... and .... me at the best restaurants.
8 The old house has gone to .... and .... now. I can't afford to restore it.
9 It's a good course; you can .... and .... which classes you want to attend.
10 There are a lot of .... and .... to discuss before we finish the meeting, but there's nothing major or very important.

72.3

10 marks

Some of these binomials are correct, others are the wrong way round. Reverse the words in the incorrect ones.

Example: Foremost and first, I'd like to introduce our main guest tonight.
　　　　　First and foremost ...

1 It was nice to have some peace and quiet after the children left.
2 The doctor said I should get some recreation and rest.
3 I've been driving forth and back to London every day for the last three weeks.
4 There are car parks here and there in the city centre. Just look out for the signs.
5 My feet are tired. I've been going fro and to all morning.
6 He ran up and down the street looking for her.
7 He was out and down in Los Angeles for a year, then he got a job and an apartment.
8 She was in bed ill for two weeks, but now she's out and about again.
9 I wanted a white and black film, not a colour film.
10 The cheapest rooms, with no water, were 10 dollars a night. For an extra five dollars you could have a room with cold and hot water.

72.4

10 marks

Fill the gaps in these binomials with *or*, *to* and *but*.

1 Slowly .... surely, my English got better as I studied and practised.
2 Sooner .... later I will have to buy a car. I can't go on getting taxis every day.
3 With John, it's always all .... nothing. There are no compromises or half measures.
4 Do you realise you've got your sweater on back .... front?
5 She'll have to learn to sink .... swim; she can't always depend on everyone else to solve her problems for her.

Your score

/40

TEST
73 Idioms describing people

73.1
10 marks
Fill the gaps with words from the box. The expressions in the left-hand column are more or less opposite in meaning to those in the right-hand column.

top	odd	heart	cold	mover	slow	quick	coach	middle	hard

1 He has a .... of gold.
3 She was .... off the mark and got there first.
5 He's a fast ....
7 She's very ....-of-the-road.
9 He's a bit over the .... when you first meet him.

2 He's as .... as nails.
4 She was a bit .... off the mark and arrived too late.
6 He's a bit of a slow-............... .
8 She's a bit of an ....-ball.
10 He's rather a .... fish when you first meet him.

73.2
10 marks
Now match the completed sentences in 73.1 above to these sentences with the same meaning.

a She's rather eccentric.
b She was not quick enough.
c He's very exaggerated in his behaviour.
d He always takes ages to do everything.
e He's a wonderfully kind person.
f She's rather moderate in her views and behaviour.
g He is very tough and is not easily moved by anything.
h She reacted quickly and benefited from it.
i He's very formal and a bit unfriendly.
j He always does everything in super-quick time.

73.3
10 marks
Place the expressions into one of the columns to show their meaning.

awkward customer	round the bend	as good as gold
pain in the neck	gets on everyone's nerves	

nuisance/difficult person	nice person	crazy/mad person

73.4
10 marks
Put a plus sign (+) if the expression is a positive way of describing someone, and put a minus sign (−) if the expression is a negative one. (*5 marks*)

the teacher's pet ( )   top of the class ( )   a know-all ( )   a big-head ( )   a lazy-bones ( )

Now use the expressions to fill the gaps.

1 At school she was always .... , in fact, in one exam, she scored 100 per cent.
2 George is such a .... He always has the right answer, or thinks he does.
3 She's a bit of a .... If she can avoid working, she will.
4 It's not nice to be .... All the other students make fun of you.
5 What a .... She really thinks she's wonderful, doesn't she!

Your score /40

TEST
74 Idioms describing feelings or mood

74.1 Divide these idioms into two groups: *positive* feelings/moods, and *negative* feelings/moods.
10 marks Put a plus sign (+) for positive, and a minus sign (−) for negative.

1 I was on cloud nine all day. ( )
2 The boss was in a really black mood this morning. ( )
3 He's been going round like a bear with a sore head all day. ( )
4 Everyone seems to be in high spirits tonight. ( )
5 I felt browned off with the situation. ( )
6 She seems to be keeping her chin up. ( )
7 You're looking down in the dumps. What happened? ( )
8 He had a face as long as a fiddle. ( )
9 Lily's as happy as the day is long. ( )
10 She was over the moon when she heard the news. ( )

74.2 Match the 10 idioms (1–10) with the 10 explanations (a–j) below.
10 marks

♊ **Gemini** You'll feel (1) **as pleased as Punch** and you'll be (2) **on top of the world** for most of the day. But (3) **don't get carried away**, because you could (4) **feel a bit down** because of something that happens in the evening.

Taurus You'll (5) **be on the edge of your seat** most of the day waiting for something big to happen, but (6) **keep a cool head**. You'll (7) **be in two minds** over an invitation, but take your time before you decide.

♎ **Libra** Something (8) **makes you swell with pride**, but in the afternoon (9) **you'll be up in arms** over something that happens at work. (10) **You've had itchy feet** for the last week or two, so start planning that holiday now!

a You feel very proud indeed.
b You must not lose touch with reality.
c You must stay calm.
d You feel totally elated.
e You feel restless and want to travel.
f You feel very angry/enraged.
g You feel a little depressed.
h You are in a state of suspense.
i You cannot decide.
j You are very pleased with yourself.

74.3 Fill the gaps to complete the meaning in brackets. You are given the first letter.
20 marks

Example: I felt as though my head was going r.*ound*.. . (dizzy)

1 I'm feeling a.............. in. (very tired/exhausted)
2 I could see he was s.............. stiff. (very frightened)
3 I was almost at death's d.............. last week; but I'm better now. (very ill)
4 My uncle is 88 but he's as f.............. as a fiddle. (in excellent physical condition)
5 I'm so hungry I could eat a h.............. ! (very hungry indeed)
6 I'm feeling a bit under the w.............. today. (not very well)
7 Don't come up behind me like that. You frightened the l.............. out of me! (gave me a fright)
8 I j.............. out of my skin when the explosion happened. (had a very sudden fright)
9 The poor boy was shaking in his s.............. . (trembling with fear)
10 She was on t.............. form in the Olympic Games last year. (at her best performance)

Your score
/40

TEST
75 Idioms describing problematic situations

75.1

10 marks

Complete the idiomatic expressions using one of the phrases in the box.

take notice	end of the tunnel	the hatchet	a turning-point	the bottom of things
a grasp	act together	a dead end	the tide	under the carpet

1 The two sides have buried .... and have stopped arguing with each other now.
2 I'm afraid we've reached .... I just don't know what we do now to solve the problem.
3 I've been trying to get .... of these instructions but I can't make any sense of them.
4 I've sent a very strong protest letter. That should make them sit up and ....
5 The whole problem has just been swept .... Nobody has done anything about it.
6 We're going to have a full investigation to get to ....
7 At last I can see some light at the .... I think we are heading for better times.
8 .... has turned and the economy is growing again now.
9 It's time we got our .... and did something about all the complaints we've received.
10 I think we've reached .... Things are going to be different from now on.

75.2

12 marks

Arrange these idioms into three pairs of more or less opposite meaning (*2 marks per pair*).

1 lay one's cards on the table   3 keep one's cards close to one's chest   5 stir things up
2 take the bull by the horns   4 pour oil on troubled waters   6 take a back seat

Now use the pairs in these sentences.

1 I've been trying to .... , but you just ....
Why can't you leave people to try to get along with one another?
2 You should .... and do something about it. It's no good always
choosing to ....
3 I .... for a long time, but then I decided to
.... and tell her everything.

75.3

6 marks

Complete these three idioms. They all refer to difficult or problematic states or situations.

be in a ⟨
f.................   (in difficulty)
m.................   (in a state of confusion)
t .... corner   (situation that is difficult to get out of)

75.4

12 marks

Match the six idioms underlined (1–6) with the six explanations (a–f) below.

1 We had to go back to square one.
2 Politics and money go hand in hand in this country.
3 I was on tenterhooks yesterday waiting to hear if I'd passed the exam.
4 An apology would go a long way. Why don't you try?
5 We're trying to find a happy medium to satisfy everybody.
6 She'd better learn to toe the line or there will be serious consequences.

a be very effective   d behave properly/obey the rules
b a compromise   e the very beginning
c in suspense   f together

Your score
/40

TEST
76 Idioms connected with praise and criticism

76.1

10 marks

Divide these idioms into two groups: those connected with praising someone/something, and those connected with criticism.
Put a plus sign (+) for praise, and a minus sign (−) for criticism.

+/−

1 (Someone) is head and shoulders above the rest   (   )
2 (Someone) is a dab hand at (something)   (   )
3 (Something) is a dog's breakfast   (   )
4 (Someone/something) is streets ahead of the rest   (   )
5 (Someone) is dressed up like a dog's dinner   (   )
6 (Someone/something) knocks spots off the rest   (   )
7 (Someone) is the world's worst   (   )
8 (Something) is out of this world   (   )
9 (Someone) wants to have their cake and eat it   (   )
10 (Someone) thinks they're the cat's whiskers   (   )

76.2

10 marks

Now use the idioms in 76.1 above to complete the sentences.

1 The restaurant is the best in town. It just ....
2 Mary is such a big-head; she really ....
3 Did you see Marlene at the party last night? She was ....
   Everyone else was looking quite informal. I wonder who she was trying to impress?
4 The teacher said my exam paper was a bit of a .... She's right. It
   was very bad. I'll have to do it again.
5 When it comes to countries with advanced technology, Japan is ....
6 Bobby doesn't want to work, but he still wants me to pay him every week. He
   .... !
7 That strawberry dessert you made was .... Absolutely delicious!
8 Jenny is .... ! You can never rely on her for anything!
9 Laura is .... at cooking Indian food. She makes some wonderful
   dishes.
10 No other child in his age group is as clever as David. He's ....

76.3

8 marks

What is a person doing if ...

1 they are buttering somebody up?
2 they are picking holes in someone else's work?
3 they want jam on it?
4 they are running down their country?

76.4

12 marks

Answer the questions. You are sometimes given the first letter of the correct answer.

1 What word rhymes with *bee's* to form an idiom with it? k........................s
2 If you *have the gift of the gab* are you (a) a good singer (b) a good talker (c) a good
   dancer?
3 If you *have a way with little children*, do they probably like you or dislike you?
4 What colour fingers do good gardeners have?
5 What adjective comes before *notch* to mean 'first-class' or 'outstanding'? t...........................
6 If you are *on the ball*, is that usually a good thing or a bad thing?

Your score

/40

TEST
77 Idioms connected with using language

77.1 Choose the best alternative, (a), (b) or (c), to explain the meaning of these idioms.

10 marks

Example: Mary got the wrong end of the stick.
Mary (a) was unfairly accused of something. (b) took something by mistake.
(c) misunderstood something.

1 I could not make head or tail of what he was telling me.
I could not (a) hear it. (b) make sense of it. (c) agree with it.
2 We were talking at cross-purposes.
We were talking (a) angrily to each other. (b) about two different things.
(c) with the same intention.
3 I couldn't get a word in edgeways with her.
I couldn't (a) say anything because she talked all the time. (b) be angry with her because I
like her. (c) convince her.
4 I know that people are talking behind my back.
I know that people are (a) criticising me when I'm not present. (b) talking in the back seat
when I'm trying to drive. (c) saying things in support of me.
5 I'm going to have to give him a talking-to.
I'm going to have to give him (a) a stern reproach. (b) some lessons. (c) a microphone.

77.2 Complete these idioms with words from the box.

30 marks

small talk	talk down	speaks her mind	talking shop	the ball rolling
sense	get to the point	to put it in a nutshell	long-winded	rubbish

1 TOM: What was the lecture like?
RICK: Oh, awful! It was really .... It lasted three hours!
2 NORA: I was amazed at how direct she was; she didn't care who she offended.
MIKE: Well, yes, she always .... and doesn't care who hears it.
3 HAZEL: Did you agree with what he said?
MEL: No, I thought he was talking complete ....
4 FRED: Did you agree with what she said?
BOB: Yes, I thought she talked a lot of ....
5 ANNA: Oh dear, the introduction's been going on for a quarter of an hour already!
FIONA: Yes, I wish he would .... and tell us why we're here.
6 DAN: So, how did the meeting start?
BOB: Well Karen started .... by reading out a long list of items to be
discussed.
7 CHRIS: Can you tell me briefly what went on at the meeting?
PAT: Well, ... , not much. But if you want all the details, I'll tell you.
8 PAUL: He said that someone with my experience would have difficulty understanding the
concept.
JANE: Don't worry. John tends to .... to people.
9 PHIL: I really think we should have a bigger budget for computer equipment. Everyone
in the finance department needs their own printer.
CLAIRE: Can we talk about something else? I hate ....
10 JIM: Did you get a chance to chat to anyone before the meeting?
MICK: Well, we had a few minutes of .... before we got down to business.

Your score
/40

Test Your English Vocabulary in Use (Upper-intermediate)

TEST
78 Miscellaneous idioms

78.1
10 marks
Each of these idioms is based on the name of a part of the human body. Fill the gap with a word from the box. The words in brackets will help you with the meaning.

head	chest	hand	nose	finger

1 You've got to .... it to him; he's a first-class tennis-player. (acknowledge/admit)
2 She's involved in millions of things. She's got a .... in every pie. (is involved in many different things)
3 I had to pay through the .... for the ticket for that concert. (pay a huge amount)
4 I've made quite a bit of ....way with my English this year. (progress)
5 I'm sorry if I've offended you with what I've just told you, but I just had to get it off my .... (confess something or tell something that has been worrying you)

78.2
10 marks
The idioms on the left are connected with paying and buying and selling. Match them with the explanations on the right.

1 buy a pig in a poke   a pay up, usually a large amount
2 pay over the odds   b charge too much; very informal
3 foot the bill   c buy something bad or defective without realising it at first
4 rip someone off   d be unwilling to negotiate over the price of something
5 drive a hard bargain   e pay more than the usual price/rate

78.3
10 marks
Fill the gaps with a word from the box.

box	feet	crash	nap	freshen

1 I'm just going to have a .... Wake me at five o'clock, will you?
2 I'm very tired. I think I'll just put my .... up tonight and watch the ....
3 The bathroom's on the left if you want to .... up.
4 I'm exhausted! I just want to .... out.

78.4
10 marks
Choose the correct explanation of the idioms in bold.

1 She **has a sharp tongue.** (a) She speaks very fast. (b) She can be very aggressive.
2 The rebel soldiers finally **came to heel.** (a) won the battle (b) agreed to obey the authorities
3 She should be made to **toe the line.** (a) behave correctly (b) walk properly
4 I **have** that song **on the brain.** (a) I can't stop singing it. (b) I've learnt it.
5 I hope you'll **back me** at the meeting. (a) speak after I do (b) support me

Your score
/40

TEST
79 Proverbs

79.1 Fill the gaps in these proverbs. You are given the first letter.

10 marks
1 Never judge a book by its c............... .
2 Take care of the pence and the p............... will take care of themselves.
3 Don't count your chickens before they are h............... .
4 Never look a gift horse in the m............... .
5 Don't put all your e............... in one basket.

79.2 Now match the proverbs (1–5) in 79.1 above with these explanations (a–e).

10 marks
a Don't anticipate the future before it happens.
b Never refuse good fortune when it is there in front of you.
c Don't invest all your efforts, or attention, in just one thing.
d Don't judge people/things by their outward appearance.
e Take care of small sums of money and they will become large sums.

79.3 These proverbs are all connected with animals and birds. Can you complete them using the
10 marks animal names from the box?

horse	bird	cat	swallow	mice

1 When the ....'s away the .... will play.
2 A .... in the hand is worth two in the bush.
3 You can lead a .... to water but you cannot make it drink.
4 One .... doesn't make a summer.

79.4 Guess the missing word based on the clues given in the pictures.

10 marks

1 There's no smoke without .... (*or* Where there's smoke, there's ....)
2 Too many .... spoil the broth.
3 People who live in .... houses shouldn't throw stones.
4 Many .... make light work.
5 Don't cross your .... before you come to them.

Your score
/40

Expressions with do and make

80.1 Put the words into the correct columns.

10 marks

a mistake	your duty	a face	your homework	a go of	a noise
a profit	the ironing	allowances	an appointment	an attempt
your worst	business with	some washing	a cake	the best of	the
gardening	your best	an excuse	war	a suggestion

make	do
a mistake	

80.2 Fill the gaps with prepositions or particles.

10 marks

Example: These sentences have been made ...up...... to illustrate how different phrasal verbs based on *do* and *make* are used.

1 Why did Bob make .... so quickly when I arrived?
2 We're doing .... our kitchen and we could do .... more paint.
3 Buying a house is expensive. We'll have to do .... a holiday this year.
4 A new house should make .... no holiday!
5 We're doing .... our very old cooker and buying a new one.
6 John sent me a note yesterday and I can't make .... what he's written.
7 We didn't have a map, so we made .... the hills hoping to find somewhere to stay.

80.3 Explain the difference between:

10 marks

1 My husband does a lot of work. / My husband makes a lot of work.
2 I'm going to do the windows today. / I'm going to make the windows today.
3 I have to do the dishes. / I have to make the dishes.
4 Joe makes a lot of washing-up. / Joe does a lot of washing-up.
5 Alex did his violin. / Alex made his violin.

80.4 Check that you have the correct answers to exercise 80.1. Then choose one of the expressions from the box in exercise 1 to complete each sentence.

10 marks

Example: I was very pleased because I _didn't make any mistakes_ in the test.

1 Emily's very good at .... a bad situation.
2 Dad's trying to sleep. Please don't ....
3 As long as you .... in the test, it doesn't matter what marks you get.
4 The business .... last year but we're afraid it won't this year.
5 Older children have to learn .... for the fact that their younger siblings are less able to do things than they are.

Your score
/40

8| Expressions with bring and take

81.1

10 marks

Underline the phrasal verbs in these sentences and suggest a synonym.

Example: She <u>brought</u> six children <u>up</u> all on her own.   *raised*

1 The government promised to bring down the cost of petrol soon.
2 Jane takes after her mother in looks but her father in temperament.
3 Although she's forty she's just taken up the guitar!
4 I wonder if they will ever bring back corporal punishment?
5 Don't be taken in by his easy charm. He's got a cruel streak.
6 Hotels often take on temporary staff in the summer.
7 They're bringing out a sequel to that novel I read on holiday last year.
8 She's trying to bring her husband round to the idea of moving to Rome.
9 I wonder if the teacher realises how well Ben can take him off.
10 We took to each other at once and speak on the phone almost daily now.

81.2

10 marks

Write sentences that mean the same but use *take* or *bring* in any form as well as the word in brackets.

Example: Psychologists are very interested in conducting research into twins who are raised in different circumstances. (bring)

> **Psychologists are very interested in conducting research into twins who are brought up in different circumstances.**

1 It's right that their affair should be made public. (open)
2 I hope they won't exploit you. (advantage)
3 His parents always seem to cope calmly with everything he does. (stride)
4 The research revealed some very interesting facts. (light)
5 We participated in a charity concert last week. (part)
6 Dick immediately started organising the situation. (charge)
7 The new rules will soon become law. (force)
8 His rudeness astounded me. (breath)
9 If you'll look after the children, I'll pop to the shops. (care)
10 I think the scandal may well cause the government to fall. (down)

81.3

20 marks

Fill the gaps with appropriate prepositions or particles.

Sophie was brought ...**up**......... in England in the country. When she was 17 she went to visit an aunt in New York. She was nervous when her flight to New York took [1].............. six hours late and the cold New York winter brought [2].............. a nasty cold. But she soon began to feel at home and was taking the city [3].............. granted. Living there really brought [4].............. the best [5].............. Sophie. She had always enjoyed taking [6].............. her teachers and now she decided to take [7].............. drama. She took part [8].............. an amateur production. She took a great pride [9].............. her performance, which was so successful that a professional drama group was keen to take her [10].............. . Although acting is a difficult career, they were sure she could bring it [11].............. . The suggestion took her breath [12].............. at first but then she decided that she had really taken [13].............. acting and wanted to make it her career. Her father couldn't take the idea [14].............. at first as he had assumed she would go for a job taking care [15].............. children. He said she had been taken [16].............. by false promises but eventually she brought him [17].............. and he took [18].............. what he had said. Her mother took it all [19].............. her stride from the start. Now Sophie's career has really taken [20].............. and she's becoming quite famous all over the world.

Your score

/40

TEST

82 Expressions with get, set and put

82.1
10 marks

Choose one of the words from the box to complete the gaps. You may use the words more than once each.

| aside | away | off | out | over | up | with |

Example: Can I help you put ..ʊᴘ.......... your tent?

1 When you've put .... your toys, we'll set .... for school.
2 He's set .... some money with a view to setting .... a business of his own one day.
3 I hope I'm not putting you .... by asking you to put me ....
4 We'll put .... our holiday until Jack has got .... the flu.
5 I don't know how you put .... his bad behaviour!

82.2
10 marks

Explain what the underlined expressions mean in this paragraph.

Example: had a family get-together   *had a family party/reunion/meeting*

Last week the Smiths <u>had a family get-together</u>. It [1]<u>got off to a bad start</u> when they started arguing about the twins' future careers. Jane [2]<u>has set her heart on becoming</u> a singer but her father is very [3]<u>set in his ways</u> and [4]<u>has put his foot down</u>. He says that she [5]<u>mustn't put all her eggs in one basket</u> and should do a secretarial course. Her twin brother John [6]<u>has set his sights on becoming</u> a Member of Parliament. He and his friends spend hours [7]<u>setting the world to rights</u>; they are convinced that, if they [8]<u>put their mind to it</u>, they would be able to [9]<u>get rid of</u> many of society's ills. His father, however, is [10]<u>set against</u> this idea too.

82.3
10 marks

Match the sentence beginnings with continuations.

1 I couldn't get through
2 I don't know how they get by
3 I had never set foot
4 It's time you got down
5 Sam's got very behind
6 They've put off the meeting
7 We could put them up
8 We should try to set off
9 You mustn't put up notices
10 You really should put in

a with his correspondence.
b for that job.
c on the walls of the school hall.
d on her wages.
e to my sister last night.
f to some revision for your exams.
g in his house before.
h until next month.
i before the rush hour.
j for tonight.

82.4
10 marks

Explain what *get* means in each of these sentences.

Example: I got this dress in the sales.   *bought*

1 I'll get dinner tonight but could you get some wine?
2 How are you getting to Jackie's party?
3 I've noticed my parents getting much older over the last few years.
4 I only got to know Julie last month but we've already got very close.
5 Why does he behave like that? I really don't get it.
6 His tuneless whistling really gets me.
7 She got First Class Honours in Classics at university.
8 Did you get the right answer to question 6?

Your score

/40

TEST
83 Expressions with come and go

83.1
10 marks

Fill in the gaps in these sentences. In sentences 1–5, use a form of either *come* or *go*. In sentences 6–10, add a preposition.

1 His tie doesn't really .... with his suit.
2 As the course .... on, I began to enjoy it more.
3 Apple trees usually .... into bloom in April in England.
4 It .... without saying that we'll give her a birthday present.
5 Please .... round and see me some time soon.
6 My alarm clock goes .... every morning at 7.15.
7 It's always hard to come .... terms with a death in the family.
8 Her jokes never quite seem to come ....
9 Although the children have been .... the go all day, they don't seem tired.
10 They went .... great lengths to make the evening a success.

83.2
10 marks

Match the underlined expressions with the definitions in the box below the text.

I hope Jim and Sarah will manage to ⁽¹⁾<u>make a go</u> of their marriage. However, I am sure no wife or family will ever ⁽²⁾<u>come between</u> Jim and his music. Ever since he ⁽³⁾<u>came across</u> an old guitar in a flea market and ⁽⁴⁾<u>had his first go</u> at playing it, Jim has been a fanatical guitarist. ⁽⁵⁾<u>It goes without saying</u> that the guitar will accompany them on their honeymoon. Jim has great hopes of ⁽⁶⁾<u>coming to an agreement</u> with a recording company but, although his playing is all right, ⁽⁷⁾<u>as far as it goes</u>, not enough people really ⁽⁸⁾<u>go for</u> his style of music at the moment and who knows if it will ever ⁽⁹⁾<u>come into fashion</u> again. Still, perhaps one day a CD of his work will ⁽¹⁰⁾<u>come out</u>.

are enthusiastic about	be published	become fashionable	found by chance
getting a contract	had his first try	it is self-evident	make a success
separate	within its limitations		

83.3
10 marks

Put these words into the appropriate category – those that collocate with *come to* and those that collocate with *come into*.

a conclusion	a decision	an end	existence	a fortune
money	one's senses	operation	a standstill	use	view

come to *a conclusion* ....
come into ....

83.4
10 marks

Correct the errors in these sentences. Note that not all of the errors are with prepositions.

Example: I wouldn't like to go ~~over~~ that experience again. **through**

1 She's absolutely trustworthy – she'd never go back on her sentences.
2 If red wine has been spilt, salt will help the stain to come away.
3 Switch on the timer so that the heating goes in an hour before we get up.
4 The history goes that they once had a relationship.
5 Many small businesses go to bankrupt every year.

Your score

/40

TEST
84 Miscellaneous expressions

84.1
10 marks

Choose a verb from the box and put it in the correct form.

break	let	look	run	see	turn

Example: It's time you ..**looked**.. for a new job.

1 We thought the car had .... down but it had just .... out of fuel.
2 .... out! Make sure you don't .... go of the rope or Harry'll fall.
3 It's my job to .... to the arrangements, so let's .... over the plans again.
4 When we were .... Anna off at the station, we .... into some old friends.
5 Katie .... down his invitation because she was .... forward to an early night.

84.2
10 marks

Use one of the expressions in the box to complete these sentences.

a good turn	broke the record	broke her heart	let it slip
looks down his nose	on the bright side	over a new leaf	run off our feet
see your way	wood for the trees	~~let go of~~	

Example: If you ..**let go of**.. her hand, she might get lost.

1 Milly says her boss sometimes can't see the ....
2 Pat is pessimistic but his wife usually looks ....
3 In January he has promised to turn ....
4 I'm worn out. We've been .... today.
5 She says that it .... when her husband died.
6 Could you possibly .... to finishing the report today?
7 He's very snobbish – he .... at most other people.
8 Richard .... that they were planning to get married.
9 My grandma used to tell me to try to do someone .... every day.
10 Jill was overjoyed when she .... for the 100m.

84.3
10 marks

Answer these questions. Give reasons for your answers.

Example: When people turn over a new leaf, are they reading? **No, they are making a resolution to behave differently in some way.**

1 Do pop singers like a large turnout at a concert?
2 If you say you're 'seeing things' do you mean you are long-sighted?
3 If you run into someone, do you hurt yourself?
4 If you ask someone to let you be, are you feeling sociable?
5 Where do you usually see someone off?

84.4
10 marks

Now answer these questions.

1 Name four things people often run out of.   **petrol** ...
2 Name four things people often look forward to.
3 Name four things that often break down.
4 Name four things that you can turn down.
5 Name four things that you can look up.

TEST
85 Formal and informal words (1)

85.1 Place these words into the appropriate column.

10 marks

~~booze~~	bike	spud	beverage	abode	potato
farewell	quid	bicycle	house	pound	

formal	neutral	informal
		booze

85.2 Give an informal alternative for the words in bold in these notices.

10 marks

Example: instead of <u>proprietors</u> in 4, write <u>owners</u>.

1
Joe's Restaurant
Only food **purchased on the premises** may be **consumed** here.

2
Do not **attempt** to **alight** while the bus is **in motion**.

3
We **regret** we do not **accept** credit cards.

4
*The **proprietors** accept no responsibility for **articles deposited** here.*

85.3 Give shorter, more informal versions of these words.

10 marks

Example: telephone **phone**

1 laboratory
2 veterinary surgeon
3 television
4 advertisement (*give two alternatives; 2 marks*)
5 the London Underground

6 mother
7 newspaper
8 goodbye
9 children

85.4 Make the <u>underlined</u> words *more formal* or *less formal*, as in the instructions in brackets.

10 marks

1 Would you like to come to my <u>house</u> for a meal? (less formal)
2 If the owner of the estate died without any <u>children</u>, the land became the property of the government. (more formal)
3 We are not allowed to bring <u>beverages</u> into the lecture room. (less formal)
4 There's a newsagent's. Shall we <u>buy</u> a newspaper? (less formal)
5 Karen is very <u>brainy</u>. She'll do well at university, I'm sure. (more formal)
6 Oh yes, Pascal is an old <u>pal</u> of mine. I've known him for years. He's a nice <u>chap</u>. (more formal; *2 marks*)
7 I had a <u>kip</u> in the afternoon, then I worked all evening. (more formal)
8 Would you like to go to a <u>public house</u> for a meal one day? (less formal)
9 He tried to <u>board</u> the train without a ticket, and got stopped by the inspector. (less formal)

Your score
/40

TEST
86 Formal and informal words (2)

86.1 Put the slang expressions in the correct category.

10 marks

~~ace~~	bread	brill	class	cool	dough	jerk	prat	readies	wally	wicked

stupid person	money	great
		ace

86.2 Answer these questions about slang.

8 marks

1 What kind of language is slang – formal or informal?
2 What is the difference between slang and colloquial language?
3 Would you ever see slang in writing?
4 Why do people use slang?
5 Money, stupid people and expressions of admiration are concepts that give rise to a lot of slang expressions. Name four other concepts that often have slang expressions. (*2 marks*)
6 As a foreign learner of English, why is it probably not a good idea for you to use slang? Give two reasons. (*2 marks*)

86.3 Identify the Cockney rhyming slang expressions in the sentences below and translate them into ordinary English. Three of the sentences each contain two expressions.

8 marks

Example: Feel like going to the rub-a-dub-dub?   *rub-a-dub-dub = pub*

1 The trouble and strife's at home looking after the Gawd forbids.
2 You've left your titfer on the Cain and Abel in the bedroom.
3 Let's have a butcher's at the lean and lurch while we're in the village?
4 My Hampstead Heath are playing me up something awful.
5 Jill fell down the apples and pears but she didn't even scratch herself.

86.4 Match the underlined expressions in this dialogue between two truck-drivers using CB radio to talk to each other to their translations in the box. Then explain why you think each underlined expression came to have this meaning.

14 marks

Example: grandma lane = slow lane (grandma = grandmother; the implication is that old ladies move slowly).

beer	children	fuel	headlights	~~slow lane~~	stolen	tyres	yes

BILL: I'm stuck in the <u>grandma lane</u>. People keep flashing their <u>eyeballs</u> at me but I'm not letting them past. They can wait till I stop for some <u>motion lotion</u>.
FRED: What're you carrying today?
BILL: A load of <u>doughnuts</u>.
FRED: <u>Five finger discount</u> ones?
BILL: No way. Can't risk anything now I've got two <u>ankle-biters</u>.
FRED: Fancy a <u>super cola</u> this evening?
BILL: <u>Affirmative</u>.

Your score

/40

TEST
87 US English

87.1

10 marks

Solve the crossword by writing the British English equivalents of the US words that form the clues.

Across
1 elevator
4 panty-hose
6 closet
9 faucet
10 vacation

Down
2 apartment
3 freeway
5 yard
7 trunk (of car)
8 diaper

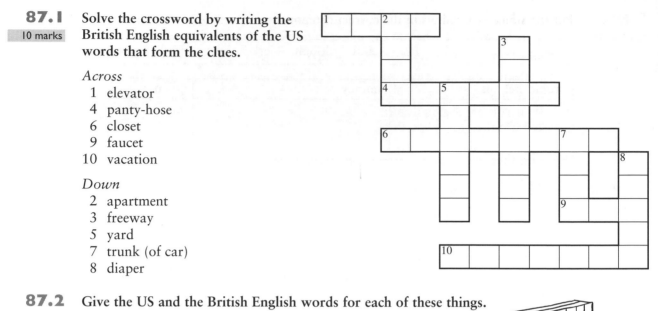

87.2

10 marks

Give the US and the British English words for each of these things.

Example:

hood (US)   bonnet (BR)

87.3

10 marks

Explain what (a) a British person and (b) someone from the USA would mean when they say:

Example: Can I have our bill, please? A British person wants to pay in a restaurant and is asking the waiter for the piece of paper which totals what they have spent. A US person is asking someone to give back a piece of paper money that belongs to them.

1 Can I have some (potato) chips, please?
2 Would you like to wash up?
3 We live on the fourth floor.
4 He's wearing a very old vest.
5 Did you use the subway to get here?

87.4

10 marks

What would someone from the US write instead of these words?

Example: film   movie

Your score

/40

1 biscuit	3 labour	5 petrol	7 rubbish	9 toilet
2 car park	4 pavement	6 modernise	8 theatre	10 torch

TEST
88 Other Englishes

88.1

What variety of English are the following statements characteristic of: Australian, Black, Indian or Scots? And what do the underlined words mean?

Example: She's a <u>bonny</u> girl. **Scots, pretty**

1 The Prime Minister is to be <u>felicitated</u> on her successful handling of the crisis.
2 Let's <u>jam</u>, <u>chicks</u>!
3 Would you like a <u>wee dram</u>?
4 What are the <u>olds</u> doing this <u>arvo</u>?

88.2

What do these typically Australian abbreviated forms mean?

Example: Aussie **Australian**

1	barbie	6	mozzie
2	beaut	7	Oz
3	biggie	8	smoko
4	journo	9	truckie
5	milko	10	uni

88.3

Divide these Scottish words into three groups – nouns that name features of the landscape, nouns for people and adjectives.

bairn	~~ben~~	bonny	brae	dreich	glen
kirk	janitor	lassie	loch	wee	

landscape	people	adjective
ben		

88.4

Match the sentence with the response.

1 Did the police nab him?
2 Did they marry in the kirk?
3 Did you have a good barbie?
4 Do you ken Shenagh?
5 Do you mind the burn?
6 How're you feeling?
7 What does he want to be?
8 What's he doing in Oz?
9 What's he like?
10 What's he look like?

a Aye, she's a bonny wee lass.
b He's got dreadlocks.
c A bit of bizzo.
d A truckie.
e It was beaut.
f No, he absconded.
g A bit of an Eve-teaser.
h Dead beat.
i The one that ran through Andy's garden?
j No, in a registry office.

TEST
89 Headline English

89.1

10 marks

What will the stories under these newspaper headlines probably be about?

Example: **MAJOR CLASH AT FORD**
A significant conflict at a Ford motor factory.

1 KEY ADVISOR QUITS
2 **FACTORY BLAST RIDDLE**
3 **STAR IN GEMS ORDEAL**
4 P M A X E S A I D
5 **MPs BACK TAX PROBE**

89.2

10 marks

Find a word from each headline which matches one of the words in the box in meaning.

Example: **TAX PROBE REVEALS FRAUD** probe = investigation

1 NEW INTEREST RATES BOOST SAVINGS
2 **FILM STAR TO WED VICAR**
3 **MORE STRIFE AT FACTORY**
4 *BY-PASS PLANS GET GO-AHEAD*
5 STORMS HIT REGION
6 *BLAZE AT LOCAL SCHOOL*
7 MOTHER'S PLEA FOR HELP
8 **HUSBAND'S FINAL VOW**
9 **PRISONERS' SECRET PLOY**
10 NEW BID TO CONQUER EVEREST

affect	approval	attempt	clever activity	conflict	encourage
fire	~~investigation~~	marry	promise	request	

89.3

10 marks

Explain the meanings of the underlined words in the headlines 1–8, then answer 9.

Example: **MAJOR <u>CLASH</u> AT FORD** clash: dispute or conflict

1 PEACE <u>MOVES</u> AT RISK
2 **TV <u>POLL</u> EXPOSED**
3 **MERGER <u>TALKS</u> FAIL**
4 COURTROOM <u>DRAMA</u> ENDS
5 *IBM <u>HEAD</u> TO GO*
6 **SON <u>OUSTS</u> DAD**
7 PRINCE <u>PLEDGES</u> SUPPORT
8 **JOBS <u>THREAT</u> AT FACTORY**

9 Why are these words used in headlines?

89.4

10 marks

Explain the pun (i.e. play on words) in these headlines.

Example: **CYMBALS CLASH** There is a pun here in that clash is a verb often used to describe the sound that the musical instrument, cymbals, make. However, clash in newspaper headlines usually means conflict and the story will probably be about some orchestral problem involving cymbalists.

1 TREE BOSS AXED
2 **MAFIA GOLF LINKS**
3 **SCHOOL'S CHOCOLATE BAR**
4 **ROAD RAGE DRIVE**
5 *TRAFFIC WARDENS CURBED*

Your score

/40

TEST
90 The language of signs and notices

90.1 Where might you see these notices and what do they mean?

10 marks

Example: out of order *The machine is not working.*

1 **NOTHING TO DECLARE**

2 **PAY AND DISPLAY**

3 **No vacancies**

4 **NO BILL-STICKING**

5 **Dogs must be carried**

90.2 Match the notice words with their more everyday meanings.

10 marks

1	prosecute	a	means of transport
2	penalty	b	get off (bus or train)
3	trespasser	c	someone who is not yet legally an adult
4	refrain	d	take to court
5	prohibit	e	buy or something bought
6	alight	f	get off (horse or bike)
7	minor	g	punishment
8	purchase	h	not to do something
9	vehicle	i	someone who goes on private land without permission
10	dismount	j	forbid

90.3 Put the words in order to make typical notices. What does each one mean?

20 marks

Example: the / walking / grass / on / no   *No walking on the grass. People must keep to the paths and not tread on the grass.*

1 spoken / here / Spanish
2 carries / packet / health / this / a / warning / government /
3 prohibited / animals / feeding / strictly / the
4 holders / only / admission / to / permit
5 the / smoking / from / auditorium / in / refrain / kindly
6 fine / up / penalty / dropping / for / £100 / to / litter
7 minors / admission / no / to / unaccompanied
8 today / sale / starts / clearance
9 it / bus / motion / the / not / in / alight / do / whilst / is / from
10 be / shop-lifters / prosecuted / will

Your score

/ 40

Key

Test 1

1.1
1 the
2 English
3 questions *or* answers
4 of *or* about *or* in
5 carefully *or* then
6 knowledge *or* vocabulary
7 think *or* is
8 the aim of this book *or* in the back of the book *or* your knowledge of English vocabulary (for example)
9 either of the 2 sentences (The first one begins with *The* and ends with *vocabulary* and the second one begins with *Think* and ends with *book*.)
10 Possible collocations include test knowledge, think carefully and check answers.

`10 marks`

1.2 1 .   2 '   3 ?   4 -   5 :

`5 marks`

1.3
1 brackets
2 comma
3 exclamation mark
4 semi-colon
5 inverted commas

`5 marks`

1.4
1 prefix = dis
root = organis(e)
suffix = ation (3 marks)
2 5 syllables
lab is the stressed syllable (2 marks)
3 noun = width
verb = widen
adjective = wide
adverb = widely (4 marks)
4 synonym = broad
antonym = narrow (2 marks)
5 guy *or* chap *or* bloke = colloquial words for 'man' (1 mark)
6 main verb = has
subject = English
object = a very large vocabulary (3 marks)
7 adds is used intransitively
express is used transitively (2 marks)
8 pig-headed is the pejorative (or negative) word (1 mark)
9 We use informal language when we are talking to people whom we know well, and with whom we have an equal relationship. (1 mark)
10 A collocation is a set of words that are frequently associated together e.g. shades of meaning. (1 mark)

`20 marks`

Test 2

2.1
1 painter	5 writer	8 projector
2 doctor	6 worker	9 printer
3 actor	7 supervisor	10 pencil-sharpener
4 sailor		

2.2
1 pollution	5 complication	8 donation
2 impression	6 reduction	9 explanation (note spelling)
3 alteration	7 addition	10 promotion
4 admission		

2.3   1 a pianist   2 a Marxist   3 the addressee   4 a typist   5 an employee

2.4   1 sadness   2 happiness   3 craziness   4 hopelessness   5 readiness

2.5   1 refusal   2 forgetful   3 commercialise   4 excitement   5 scarcity

Test 3

3.1
1 many	5 half	8 wrongly
2 before	6 small	9 again
3 against	7 one	10 under
4 false		

3.2
1 immature	5 disapproves	8 irreplaceable
2 unreliable	6 dishonest	9 dislike
3 unwrapping	7 inconvenient	10 inedible
4 illegible		

3.3   Although Jim [(1)]used to be a soldier, he's only [(2)]partly literate (partly able to read and write). When he tries to write a letter, he [(3)]spells half the words incorrectly and his wife has to [(4)]write it again for him. His wife used to work in a [(5)]not very important department of the post office where her main job was [(6)]forwarding mail to new addresses. Jim's very [(7)]much in favour of the army but he [(8)]gives too much emphasis to its good points. His wife, on the other hand, is rather [(9)]against the army and she [(10)]doesn't give enough value to its positive aspects.

3.4   1 inedible: the prefix here means *not* whereas in the other words it means *in*
2 dissimilar: it is an adjective whereas the other words are verbs
3 uncomfortable: it is an adjective whereas the other words are verbs
4 ex-wife: the prefix here means former whereas in the other words it means *out of*
5 reasonable: its negative is formed with the prefix *un-* whereas the other words form their negative with *ir-*

Test 4

4.1   1 was / has been / is / will be / is being postponed
2 advertisements / adverts
3 supportively
4 diversion
5 introductory

4.2

verb	person noun	adjective	abstract noun
oppress	oppressor	oppressive	oppression
prospect	prospector	prospective	prospect
produce	producer	productive	production
compose	composer	composite	composition
deport	deportee	deported	deportation
convert	convert	converted	conversion

`16 marks`

4.3 2 a   3 d   4 f   5 c   6 b   `5 marks`

4.4
1 imports
2 a suspect
3 a conductor
4 introspective/introverted
5 to convert
6 introduction
7 depressing
8 an inspector
9 to depose

`9 marks`

Test 5

5.1

-ment	-ion	-ness	-ship	-ity	-dom	-hood	-th
achievement excitement	combination imagination recognition	friendliness tenderness ugliness	friendship membership ownership	complexity generosity prosperity	freedom wisdom	adulthood motherhood	depth width

`10 marks`

5.2
1 satisfaction
2 relationship
3 sensitivity
4 happiness
5 humour
6 retirement
7 kindness
8 equality
9 boredom
10 carelessness

`10 marks`

5.3 *pleasant:* improvement, brotherhood, companionship, faith, luck, calm
unpleasant: hostility, rage, bitterness, fear   `10 marks`

5.4 *Possible answers:*

-ment	-ion	-ness	-ship	-ity	-dom	-hood	-th
investment replacement	collection illusion	aggressiveness emptiness	apprenticeship partnership	anonymity curiosity	stardom kingdom	sisterhood neighbourhood	breadth strength

Abstract nouns that do not have a suffix: chance, speed, thought, reason

Check in a dictionary if you thought of words not mentioned in this key.

`10 marks: ½ mark per word`

Test 6

6.1
1 pink
2 controlled
3 top
4 minded
5 free
6 new
7 world
8 up
9 proof
10 haired

`10 marks`

6.2   tax-free
straight / blonde / short-haired (dark-haired is also possible)
blue / dark / round-eyed
first-class / hand / rate   10 marks

6.3   air-conditioned rooms   cut-price goods   built-up areas
time-consuming work   far-fetched ideas   well-off middle classes
open-necked shirt   long-distance phone calls / runner
all-out strike   off-peak phone calls   10 marks

6.4   1 big-headed man: man with a high opinion of himself
2 worn-out coat: a coat that has been worn so much that it is falling to pieces
3 never-ending lecture: a lecture that seems to go on for ages (probably because it is rather tedious)
4 quick-witted mind: intelligent mind
5 two-faced behaviour: hypocritical behaviour
6 open-toed shoes: shoes that leave the feet open to the air at the front
7 rosy-cheeked child: a child with healthy pink cheeks
8 last-minute decision: a decision that was taken just at the very last opportunity
9 part-time job: a job that does not involve working the usual full hours
10 easy-going personality: a relaxed nature

10 marks: ½ mark for each correct order; ½ mark for each explanation

Test 7

7.1   1 food   6 traffic
2 book   7 mail
3 burglar   8 road
4 race   9 wind
5 mother   10 tax   10 marks

7.2   1 Blood pressure is what the doctor measures to check on how efficiently the heart is pumping and a blood donor is a person who gives blood in order to help someone who needs a transfusion.
2 Kitchen scissors are scissors which are used in the kitchen and nail scissors are used for cutting nails.
3 Sunglasses are glasses which people wear to protect their eyes in bright sunlight and wine glasses are glasses from which people drink wine.
4 A pen-name is another word for a pseudonym and a pen-knife is another word for a pocket knife.
5 Human being means one person and human race refers to all people as a group   10 marks

7.3   baby sitter   greenhouse effect
contact lens   trademark
youth hostel   hay fever
birth control *or* birthmark   tin opener
grass roots   package holiday   10 marks

7.4   1 attack   5 state   8 barrier
2 stop   6 rights   9 wipers
3 account   7 force   10 drain   10 marks
4 penalty

Test 8

8.1 1 f 2 i 3 e 4 k 5 b 6 h 7 a 9 j 10 g 11 c   10 marks

8.2 1 out; out   4 over; out
2 out; up   5 out, by
3 out; up (*or* down)   10 marks

8.3 1 break-up / of their marriage
2 a daily / workout
3 surprisingly large (big) / turnout
4 feedback / on new initiatives
5 the outbreak / of war
6 a setback / because of the weather
7 hold-up / for (with) trains
8 an interesting write-up / of the incident
9 break-in / at our neighbour's house
10 a very unusual / layout

20 marks: 2 marks per sentence;
1 mark for each part of the phrase

Test 9

9.1

Food	Clothes and materials	Society
aubergine	anorak	ghetto
cuisine	caftan	guerrilla
yoghurt	yashmak	coup
gateau		

10 marks

9.2 1 cruise   6 karate
2 crèche   7 confetti
3 siesta   8 chauffeur
4 cul de sac   9 fiasco
5 blitz   10 avant-garde   10 marks

9.3 1 carafe   5 ski   8 mosquito
2 igloo   6 duvet   9 tattoo
3 easel   7 shawl   10 cosmonaut
4 mattress   10 marks

9.4 1 tycoon: the others are animals but a tycoon is an important business person
2 judo: the others relate to music while judo is a martial art
3 patio: the others relate to geographical features while a patio is part of a garden
4 marmalade: the others are dogs while marmalade is a kind of orange jam
for spreading on bread
5 sauna: the others are places where things can be bought while a sauna is
a place where you can go to subject your body to high temperatures
(usually with steam)
10 marks: 2 marks each

Test 10

10.1
1 The United Nations
2 care of
3 as soon as possible
4 Member of Parliament
5 Road
6 depart(s) *or* departure
7 compact disk
8 Identification/identity document or card
9 Please reply (French: Répondez s'il vous plaît)
10 arrive(s) *or* arrival

10 marks

10.2
1 laboratory
2 refrigerator (note the spelling: no *d*)
3 examination
4 representative
5 advertisement
6 paper
7 case
8 laces
9 watch
10 TV *or* (more informal) telly

10 marks

10.3

To: John Furness
From: Sally Oldbeck

Dear John,

Here are the times for my trip: **arrive** from Paris 2.25 **in the afternoon** (Latin *post meridiem*) at Victoria Station, **Wednesday** 14th. Stay with friends, **telephone:** 41356787, address 56 Carlton **Avenue**, Eastcheap, London S4. **Depart Saturday** 17th from Heathrow, flight **number** EI 654 to Dublin.
If you need to ring me in the office, it's *Orient Imports Limited,* tel 3546659, **extension** 5656.

Sally

10 marks

10.4
1 It is a digital camera, **i.e.** it doesn't use film, but takes pictures electronically.
2 I needed some paper, envelopes, pens, **etc.**
3 There are several ways of solving the problem, **e.g.** try fitting new batteries.
4 You can repair it yourself. **N.B.** the guarantee is no longer valid if you do.
5 She saw a **UFO** in the sky above her house.
6 Her address is: Flat **no** 3, Block B, Horley **St**, Bartsow.
7 She got a **BSc** from London University, and now she's doing a **PhD.**
8 There was a **PS** at the end of the letter.

10 marks: 1 mark for each item in bold

Test 11

11.1
1 audio book
2 cybercafé
3 surfing the net
4 mouse potato
5 teleshopping
6 in-line skating
7 road rage
8 waitperson
9 video jockey
10 snowboarding

10 marks

11.2   2 f   3 d   4 a   5 b   6 e

10 marks: 2 marks each

11.3
1 False. They like to see natural environments and wild life on their holidays.
2 False. They may be extremely thin if they are, for example, anorexic.
3 True
4 False. They are programmes about the everyday lives of ordinary people.
5 False. A spin doctor studies public relations rather than medicine.
6 False. It means dealing with one's banking affairs by using a computer.

7 False. Such a person is very good-looking.

8 False. Computer enthusiasts travel into cyberspace.

9 False. On a bad-hair day everything goes wrong. Going to the hairdresser's may help you feel better but it is not necessarily your hair that is the problem on a bad-hair day.

10 True

10 marks: ½ mark only, if you put false but could not explain why

11.4 1 My boss is afraid of Internet technology and always insists on using the traditional postal system.

2 People who are addicted to shopping often spend a fortune shopping via the Internet or television.

3 While I was moving rapidly from one TV channel to the next last night, I found a very interesting documentary about life in a busy café where the camera filmed people without their being aware of it.

4 Illness caused by working in an unhealthy building and psychological stress caused by a feeling of being overloaded with too much information are two of the health hazards of life in the twenty-first century.

5 He aspires to be a director and he's planning his first film – it's to be about the idolisation of Princess Diana.

10 marks

Test 12

12.1 1 doubt   3 fasten   5 hiccough   7 kneel   9 muscle (*or* mussel)
2 plough   4 psychic   6 recipe   8 sword   10 tough

10 marks

12.2 though and toe   chalk and fork   love and dove
through and blue   sorry and lorry   drove and stove
palm and arm   worry and hurry   friend and bend
fiend and leaned

10 marks

12.3 1 <u>exports</u>?   6 <u>permit</u>
2 con<u>flict</u>ing   7 re<u>cord</u>ed
3 <u>prog</u>ress   8 de<u>sert</u>
4 in<u>creas</u>es   9 <u>prot</u>est
5 per<u>mit</u>   10 <u>in</u>sult!

10 marks

12.4 Julie, a friend I met at my psychology class, left the silver com<u>b</u> I gave her for Chris<u>t</u>mas in the cas<u>t</u>le when we spent an <u>h</u>our there last week. She took it out of her bag because she wanted to get some <u>k</u>nots out of her hair while we were having a wa<u>l</u>k round the old tom<u>b</u>s there. I told her she wou<u>l</u>d lose it if she wasn't careful. And she did! Fortunately, an <u>h</u>onest person picked it up and returned it to the gatekeeper. Julie feels very inde<u>b</u>ted to that anonymous person as she was very fond of that com<u>b</u>.

10 marks: NB: only one mark for comb although it is in the text twice

Test 13

13.1 1 clashing cymbals   7 peeping car horn
2 creaking stairs   8 sizzling bacon
3 drizzling rain   9 spurting fountain
4 grunting pigs   10 tinkling bicycle bell
5 mooing cows   11 whirring propellers
6 neighing horses

10 marks

13.2
1	mash	6	sprinkled
2	splashing	7	dash
3	click	8	whistle
4	groaned	9	clinked
5	clanging	10	grunted

10 marks

13.3
1 something unpleasant or miserable: growl, grumpy
2 a sharp metallic sound: clank, clip-clop
3 movement of water: spray, spit
4 movement of air: wheeze, whistle
5 fast, violent movement: smash, crash
6 something light and repeated: trickle, crackle

Two possible examples are given for each sound. Check any others you may have thought of in a dictionary. Allow yourself the mark if they seem to have the association suggested.

10 marks: 1 mark per match; $\frac{1}{2}$ mark per example

13.4
1	rustle	6	clink
2	gargle	7	spit
3	whack	8	whip
4	growl	9	moo
5	gash	10	wheeze

Test 14

14.1 Homophones: be (bee); seen (scene); there (their / they're); two (too / to); rolls (roles); need (knead / kneed) (5 marks)

Homographs: lead (metal) and lead (to guide); row (noise) and row (line) or to row (a boat); to live (e.g. in Cambridge) and live (not recorded); pen (to write with) and pen (to keep animals in); house (a building) and to house (to give a home to) (5 marks)

10 marks

14.2
1	grinned	6	nose
2	found	7	mooned
3	I've	8	choose, juice (2 marks)
4	bed	9	now
5	no		

10 marks

14.3
1	grown, groan	6	allowed, aloud
2	hoarse, horse	7	peal, peel
3	tyre, tire	8	waist, waste
4	whine, wine	9	rain, rein
5	pail, pale	10	sort, sought

10 marks

14.4
1 A *tee* is a golfing term and *tea time* is an everyday phrase.
2 The normal expression is *love at first sight*, and site is the word used to describe the place where an archaeological dig takes place.
3 The normal phrase is *heaven sent*, and scent is another word for perfume.
4 Plaice and sole are two different kinds of fish.
5 *Sale of the century* is a phrase sometimes used in publicity to describe a spectacular sales event in a shop. When you go on a voyage, you are sailing.

10 marks

Test 15

15.1   1 c   2 c   3 b   4 c   5 c   **10 marks: 2 marks each**

15.2
1	with a view to	4	providing
2	unless	5	owing to
3	Throughout	6	Supposing

                                                                                           6 marks

15.3
1. Computers will bring about even more/even greater/even bigger changes in our lives in the new millennium.
2. There was a 20% increase in taxes. This sparked off serious riots and protests. *or:* Serious riots and protests were sparked off by the 20% increase in taxes. *or* The 20% increase in taxes sparked off …
3. He acknowledged that he had made a mistake.
4. The decision was unpopular and gave rise to a lot of angry debate.
5. This feeling of insecurity among the staff arises from a lack of communication between employers and employees.
6. Growing economic prosperity has led to great changes in family life.
7. The present problems stem from a decision made ten years ago.   **14 marks: 2 marks each**

15.4
1	conditions	3	outcome	5	circumstances
2	prompted	4	requirements		

                                                                               10 marks: 2 marks each

Test 16

16.1
1	… But for all that, …	6	… Furthermore, …
2	In addition to …	7	Apart from …
3	After all, …	8	… Besides, …
4	Admittedly, …	9	… Likewise, …
5	… but equally …	10	… Further to …

                                                                              10 marks

16.2
1. The flights get booked up very quickly. What's more, we'll have to book before the 25th to get the cheap ticket.
2. That shop sells pens, paper, you know, greetings cards, and so on.
3. She has an MA in economics. In addition, she has *or* She also has a diploma in politics.
4. It's always difficult to admit (that) I was / you were wrong.
5. I concede that I may not understand all the details, but I still think I am right in general.   **10 marks: 2 marks per sentence**

16.3   1 to   2 with   3 On   4 from   5 On   6 On   **6 marks**

16.4
1. He is a painter as well as a poet/as well as being a poet.
2. Her brother went to university, and she did too *or* and she did likewise. *or* … likewise, so did she.
3. OK, so you want to work to pay for your ticket. That's all well and good, but how are you going to find a job?
4. You need a good guide book. In addition, you need up-to-date maps and good equipment.
5. I'm not tired. Quite the opposite! I'm ready to work all night if necessary.   **10 marks: 2 marks per sentence**

16.5
1	poles apart	3	huge discrepancy
2	world of difference	4	yawning gap

                                                                                   4 marks

Test 17

17.1
  1 dilemma
  2 approach
  3 topic
  4 situation/position
  5 question/issue
  6 response
  7 solution
  8 position
  9 aspect
  10 issue/dilemma
`10 marks`

17.2
  1 point   2 position   3 view   4 key   5 claim
`10 marks`

17.3
  1 There is no way out of the situation.
  2 D'you think we'll find a solution to the problem?
  3 What was her reaction to the claim that it was her fault?
  4 Your judgement of the situation is a bit naive, if I may say so.
  5 What is your attitude to/towards the issue of private versus public schools?
`5 marks`

17.4
  1 b   2 c   3 a   4 e   5 d
`10 marks: 2 marks per item`

17.5
  1 a reaction   2 a fact   3 a claim   4 a belief   5 a fact
`5 marks`

Test 18

18.1
  1 let me see / hang on
  2 Well
  3 You see
  4 Now then
  5 Hang on!; Look
  6 So; OK; Great
  7 Mind you
`10 marks: 1 mark per gap`

18.2

1 b	6 a	11 b
2 c	7 a	12 a
3 b	8 b	13 c
4 a	9 b	14 a
5 c	10 c	15 c

`15 marks`

18.3
  1 well then   2 hang on   3 mind you   4 now then   5 you see
`5 marks`

18.4
  1 Where was I?   3 Right then!   5 You see
  2 At the end of the day   4 sort of / kind of
`10 marks`

Test 19

19.1
  1 First/Firstly/First of all
  2 Turning
  3 In parenthesis
  4 In conclusion
  5 Next
  6 Leaving aside
  7 To sum up
  8 Thirdly
  9 Briefly
  10 Secondly
`10 marks`

19.2
  1 (a) firstly   (b) first of all
  2 lastly
  3 To conclude
  4 (a) in summary   (b) in sum
  5 in sum
  6 for instance
  7 overleaf
  8 True
  9 True
`22 marks: 2 marks per correct answer`

19.3
  1 reference
  2 following
  3 see
  4 earlier
  5 further
  6 refer
  7 above
  8 other
`8 marks: 1 mark per gap`

Test 20

20.1

		uncountable	countable
1	passport	☐	✓
2	currency	✓	☐
3	luggage	✓	☐
4	reservation	☐	✓
5	accommodation	✓	☐
6	flight	☐	✓
7	information	✓	☐
8	travel	✓	☐
9	visa	☐	✓
10	journey	☐	✓

10 marks

20.2

1 We're going to the shops tomorrow. I want to look at some new **furniture**, Dan needs new clothes, Maria wants to look at skiing **equipment** and Sheila needs some **paper** for her computer printer. We'll probably spend lots of **money**!

2 After some courses, he found that he was making **progress** and increasing his **knowledge** of geography. He looked forward to continuing his studies at university and, perhaps, one day, doing some advanced **research** into the geography of his local area.

3 I really need some **advice** from you before I take up the violin. Do you have any tips about buying an instrument? Are there any works by famous composers that are easy for a beginner? Which kinds of **music** would you recommend? Any **information** you can give me would be useful.

10 marks: 1 mark for each mistake you find

20.3

flour   fish   cooking-oil   fruit   toast   garlic   parsley
soya-sauce   rice   wheat

10 marks

20.4

1 stone; stones
2 cloth; cloths
3 coal; coals
4 leather; plastic
5 glass; glasses

10 marks: 2 marks per sentence

Test 21

21.1

1	binoculars	✓	9	corkscrews	☐
2	trousers	✓	10	e-mails	☐
3	slippers	☐	11	headquarters	✓
4	pants	✓	12	pyjamas	✓
5	sunglasses	✓	13	shears	✓
6	gloves	☐	14	rulers	☐
7	tongs	✓	15	swimming trunks	✓
8	tweezers	✓			

10 marks

21.2

1 acoustics
2 authorities
3 contents
4 whereabouts
5 goods

10 marks: 2 marks per sentence

21.3

1 jodhpurs
2 glasses
3 knickers/pants
4 goggles
5 pliers
6 scissors
7 shorts
8 handcuffs
9 headphones
10 kitchen scales

10 marks

21.4

1 is   2 was; was; it   3 is; it   4 is; is; it   5 are

10 marks: 1 mark per item

Test 22

22.1
1 glass
2 cloth
3 a chocolate / some chocolates
4 fish/chicken
5 an iron
6 a wood
7 a chicken / some chickens
8 paper
9 glasses

22.2 1 S/P   2 S/P   3 S   4 S   5 P

22.3
1 **Pepper** is a powder you sprinkle over your food; **a pepper** is a vegetable.
2 **Tape** is any long, thin material (e.g. for sticking things); **a tape** usually refers to an empty or recorded cassette or reel of audio or video tape.
3 **Rubber** is the material used in car tyres; **a rubber** is an eraser, used for rubbing out things written in pencil.
4 **Coffee** is a plant or beans or a powder; **a coffee** usually means one cup of coffee.
5 **Trade** is buying and selling things (e.g. international trade); **a trade** means a type of work such as that of an electrician, plumber or carpenter, which is learnt on the job.

22.4
1 *Peoples* usually means 'different nations/cultures'.
2 *A home* usually means an institution (e.g. an old people's home) or somewhere where you can live if you have nowhere (e.g. This little dog needs a home and lots of love).
3 *Lands* means 'different countries'.
4 *Iron* means a very hard, strong material.
5 *A paper* with *a* usually means a newspaper, or an academic article or report of research.

Test 23

23.1
1 flock; herd
2 shoals
3 swarm
4 packs
5 gang; team
6 crowd; group
7 deck (you can also use 'pack' with cards: a pack of cards)

23.2
1 There is a **range** of hills and a **clump** of trees.
2 There is a **pair** of chimneys.
3 This is a **set** of drums.
4 A man sitting at a desk with a **stack** of papers.
5 This is a **row** of houses.

23.3 1 staff   2 crew   3 cast   4 public   5 company

23.4
1 a stack of (six) tables
2 a bunch of flowers
3 a heap of dirty clothes
4 a set of (six) wine glasses
5 a barrage of complaints *or* a string of complaints
6 a string of allegations
7 a whole host of questions *or* a series of questions
8 a herd of elephants
9 a flock of birds
10 a pack of wolves

Test 24

24.1
1 stroke	4 articles	7 means
2 breath	5 spots	8 gust
3 lumps	6 puffs	9 loaves; carton

24.2
1 two bars of chocolate
2 three tubes of toothpaste
3 two slices of bread
4 two bars of soap
5 three items of clothing: tights, a T-shirt and a pair of shorts

24.3
1 a state of emergency	4 a state of confusion
2 a state of flux	5 a state of uncertainty
3 a state of disrepair	6 a state of agitation

24.4 Before visiting England, let me give you some <u>pieces / bits of advice</u> and some <u>bits / pieces of information</u>. Don't take too <u>many pieces / bits of luggage</u> with you but take some warm <u>items / articles of clothing</u>. You never know whether you are going to <u>get a spell of good weather</u> or not. One day you <u>have rumbles / claps of thunder</u>, <u>flashes of lightning</u> and <u>showers of rain</u>, the next it is sunny.

(Note that the text as it is above sounds very unnatural. It would be extremely unusual to use so many of these words for making uncountable words countable in one short text.)

Test 25

25.1
1 bucket (pail)	5 jug	8 basket
2 pan (saucepan)	6 sack	9 barrel
3 bowl	7 mug	10 jar
4 tin (can)		

25.2
1 A bottle of milk is one glass (or occasionally plastic) container of milk holding a pint or a litre and a crate of milk is a wooden, metal or plastic container which holds twelve or twenty bottles upright.
2 A pot is much smaller than a tub; pots are often found indoors whereas tubs are always outdoors.
3 A packet of cigarettes contains 20 cigarettes and a carton contains ten packets of cigarettes i.e. 200 cigarettes.
4 A tube of paint would be used by an artist who would squeeze paint out of it and a tin of paint would be used by a painter and decorator. A tin of paint holds much more than a tube – often two litres.
5 A shopping bag is flexible (made of cloth or plastic) and a shopping basket is solid (made of cane or, in a supermarket, metal).
6 You eat a serving of ice-cream from a bowl (usually ceramic) and you buy a larger amount of ice-cream in a tub (made of treated card or plastic).
7 A cup of tea requires a saucer and a mug of tea does not have a saucer and holds more than most cups.
8 A pot of ointment is a kind of round jar into which you dip your finger when you need to use the ointment whereas a tube of ointment has to be squeezed to get the ointment out.

9 A box of sweets is made of card and is what you might buy as a gift for someone and a jar of sweets is made of glass and is more the kind of thing that you keep at home and fill with sweets when you buy them.

10 A jewellery box is a box where a woman keeps all her jewels whereas a jewellery case is something made specifically for one item.

20 marks: 2 marks per answer; 1 mark if only one part of the pair is described accurately

25.3

a box of	a jar of
chocolates	honey
crayons	instant coffee
matches	jam
pins	olives
tea bags	
tools	

10 marks

The strongest collocations here are, probably, box of chocolates, box of matches and jar of jam.

Test 26

26.1 Group A: -ish adjectives: Irish Danish
Group B: -ic adjectives: Arabic Icelandic
Group C: -(i)an adjectives: Brazilian Ukrainian
Group D: -i adjectives: Israeli Iraqi
Group E: -ese adjectives: Japanese Portuguese

10 marks

26.2

noun	adjective	change
Peru	Peruvian	add 'v'
Canada	Canadian	pronunciation /kəˈneɪdɪən/ change
Norway	Norwegian	change spelling to 'eg', stress and pronunciation /nɔːˈwiːdʒən/
Egypt	Egyptian	stress and pronunciation /ɪˈdʒɪpʃən/ change
Italy	Italian	stress change /ɪˈtælɪən/; 'y' changes to 'i'

10 marks: 2 marks per item

26.3 1 an Arab   4 a Swede
2 a Briton   5 a Spaniard
3 a Finn

5 marks

26.4 1 I think she married a **Scot**.
2 Have you ever heard **Bulgarian** music? It's really wonderful.
3 He went to work in the **Middle** East, in Jordan, I think.
4 I would like to live in **the UK** for a while to improve my English.
5 I love the colour of the **Mediterranean** Sea.

5 marks

26.5 1 (A) bilingual
2 dialects
3 Your first language or your mother tongue or your native language
4 The Philippines
5 Dutch

Test 27

27.1

cold	hot	wet/dry
frost	stifling	drought
chilly	scorching	downpour
freezing	close	flood
	heatwave	

27.2 1 snowdrifts 3 blizzard 5 drizzle 7 hail(stones) 9 mist
2 sleet 4 slush 6 shower 8 thunderstorm 10 smog

27.3 1 melts; thaws
2 mild
3 settle
4 hazy
5 breeze
6 overcast; poured
7 boiling; humid
8 storm; torrential; flooded
9 damp
10 muggy
11 hail

27.4 STRONG   WEAK

hurricane → gale → blustery winds → breeze

Test 28

28.1 1 bald; dark
2 blond; fair
3 long; curly
4 moustache; chubby
5 straight; thin

28.2 1 wavy
2 freckles
3 ginger
4 golden, reddish-brown
5 very short
6 plump
7 overweight
8 false; they are rather solidly built
9 true
10 obese
11 negative (= untidy-looking)
12 skinny
13 His hair is receding *or* He has a receding hairline.
14 their face and skin look healthy
15 it is normally only used for men

Test 29

29.1 2 j 3 h 4 k 5 c 6 e 7 b 8 d 9 g 10 i 11 a

29.2 The speaker approves of Sam, Sue and Jane.
The speaker doesn't approve of Mark, Mary, John, Amos, Anna,
Dave or Debby.

29.3 1 I don't agree. I think Sam is <u>unprincipled</u> and Sue is <u>weird.</u>
2 I don't agree. I think Mark is <u>self-assured</u> and Mary is <u>frank/open.</u>
3 I don't agree. I think John is <u>ambitious</u> but Jane is <u>bossy.</u>
4 I don't agree. I think Amos is <u>inquiring</u> and Anna is <u>innocent.</u>
5 I don't agree. I think Dave is <u>determined</u> and Debby is <u>open/frank.</u>

10 marks: 1 mark for each adjective used correctly

29.4
1 envious
2 gifted
3 relaxed
4 cruel
5 easy-going
6 sincere
7 jealous
8 eccentric
9 nosy
10 sensitive

10 marks

Test 30

30.1
1 false
2 true
3 true
4 false; it can mean both
5 true
6 false
7 true
8 true
9 false
10 true

10 marks

30.2 1 Jason and I are classmates.
2 I'm sorry, I can't stand Nancy.
3 They are partners.
4 She's fallen out with her colleagues again.
5 I think Richard is having an affair with his best friend's wife.

10 marks: 2 marks per sentence

30.3
1 get
2 eye/eye
3 up
4 to
5 elders
6 repelled
7 split
8 acquaintance
9 idolises
10 fiancée

10 marks

30.4 1 I <u>despise/look down on</u> my boss, even though most of my colleagues feel the opposite.
2 Maria's his <u>ex-girlfriend.</u> He has so many and changes them so often it's difficult to know who is who.
3 He's <u>junior</u> to her in terms of length of service, so the promotion is not surprising.
4 I <u>like/admire/respect</u> people who devote their whole life to working and studying.
5 She's <u>my best</u> friend. *or* She's a <u>very close</u> friend (of mine).

10 marks: 2 marks per sentence

Test 31

31.1
1 master bedroom (*or* main bedroom)
2 attic/loft
3 landing
4 cellar/basement
5 terrace/patio
6 drive
7 shed
8 hallway *or* hall
9 porch
10 utility room

10 marks

31.2
1 a/the remote control
2 a larder or pantry
3 a spare room or a guest (bed)room
4 A cellar usually means a place where things are stored; a basement can also mean a place where someone lives (e.g. a basement flat).
5 in the roof of a house
6 a study
7 a table mat
8 an ironing board
9 a chopping board
10 a power point (or an electrical socket or a plug)

10 marks

31.3
1 If the floor was dusty, or if someone dropped a glass and it smashed.
2 Putting inside a dustbin or waste bin, so that the contents can be lifted out in one go when it is full.
3 Opening bottles with corks, e.g. wine bottles.
4 A kitchen. It's for making small particles of food by rubbing against it (e.g. cheese or hard bread).
5 No. It's a small table mat for putting under a glass, to protect the table surface.

10 marks: 2 marks per question

31.4
1 A detached house is not joined to any other house. A semi-detached one is joined to just one other house and a terraced one is one of a row of joined houses. (3 marks)
2 A bedroom, sitting room and kitchen area in one room. (2 marks)
3 It only has one floor/storey. (1 mark)
4 A 'self-contained' flat is one where you do not share any facilities (e.g. bathroom, entrance door) with any other flat. (2 marks)
5 A cottage is a small house, usually in a village or in the countryside. A villa is a large, luxurious, detached house or a house especially built for holiday-makers. (2 marks)

10 marks

Test 32

32.1
1 I can't open the door; the handle has come off.
2 The bathroom was flooded this morning. It was terrible.
3 There has been a power cut.
4 The batteries have run out in my Walkman.
5 Our washing machine broke down last week.

10 marks: 2 marks per sentence

32.2

	leaking	chipped	dented	stained	bruised
car bumper			✓		
water-pipe	✓				
forehead					✓
dinner-plate		✓			
tablecloth				✓	

10 marks: 2 marks per tick

32.3
1 A cut is a clean break of the skin, usually with bleeding and a graze is a rough break of the skin, with redness but usually no blood.
2 Breaking it. When you twist it you strain a muscle, but do not break a bone.
3 The sink/washbasin is blocked.
4 Somebody has spilt something.
5 Because you are locked out.
6 No. It means the battery is dead and the car will not start.
7 Too early.
8 I'm sorry, I mislaid your letter.
9 Forward.
10 Yes.

`20 marks: 2 marks per sentence`

Test 33

33.1
1 erupts	3 break out	5 shake	7 casualties	9 survived
2 spreads	4 sweep	6 starve	8 victims	10 refugees

`10 marks`

33.2
1 suffered
2 damaged; injured
3 famine
4 tornado (preferable to *hurricane*, since tornadoes have tight, spiralling currents of air)
5 disasters
6 dead; wounded

`16 marks: 2 marks per gap`

33.3
1 Rabies
2 Yellow fever
3 Malaria
4 Leprosy
5 Cholera and typhoid
6 AIDS

`14 marks: 2 marks per word`

Test 34

34.1

2–5 years old	5–12/13 years old	12/13–18 years old	18+ years old
play-school nursery	junior school primary	comprehensive grammar school secondary sixth form	college university further

`10 marks`

34.2
1 True
2 False (they can be obtained only through universities)
3 True
4 True
5 False (A-levels are taken at 18 years old)
6 False (Professors are senior university teachers)
7 True
8 False (junior is usually 7/8–11/12 years old)

`8 marks`

34.3
1 resit
2 do; revising
3 pass; grades; continuous assessment; mark
4 skip
5 did

`10 marks`

34.4 1 school-leaving age
2 grant (or a scholarship; a scholarship is usually competitive)
3 state school
4 lecturer or tutor
5 evening classes

`12 marks: 2 marks per word or phrase`

Test 35

35.1 1 Union representative
2 Receptionist
3 Director
4 Personnel officer
5 Safety officer
6 Economist
7 Labourer
8 Skilled worker
9 Supervisor
10 Administrator

`10 marks`

35.2 1 Get the sack
2 Earn a living
3 Apply for a job
5 Do shift-work (*or* Do a job)
6 Be made redundant
7 Work nine-to-five
8 Take early retirement

`7 marks`

35.3
1	c	6	b	10	b
2	b	7	b	11	a
3	a	8	c	12	b
4	a	9	a	13	a
5	c				

`13 marks`

35.4 1 Work for different periods of time each week (e.g. nights one week, mornings the next week).
2 You can start and finish work any time within certain limits (e.g. start between 8am and 9.30am, finish between 4.30pm and 6.00pm).
3 A period of time off work for a woman who is expecting / has just had a new baby.
4 Not working because of an industrial dispute (e.g asking for more pay).
5 Getting a higher position in your job or profession.

`5 marks`

35.5 1 She's a workaholic; she **loves** going to work every day.
2 I feel very **ill**, so I'm on sick leave.
3 I got laid off from my job at the factory, so I **don't** work there **any more**.
4 You're so good at your job we've decided to **promote** you. *or* You're so bad at your job we've decided to **fire** you.
5 Bill's wife has just had a baby, so he's on **paternity** leave. *or* ... so she's on **maternity** leave. (You can also use the neutral word **parental** leave for both men and women.)

`5 marks`

Test 36

36.1 1 archery
2 ten-pin bowling
3 motor racing
4 scuba-diving
5 show-jumping
6 billiards/snooker/pool
7 windsurfing
8 ice hockey
9 fencing
10 javelin
11 table-tennis/ping-pong
12 high jump
13 discus
14 long jump

`14 marks`

36.2 1 a (tennis) racket
2 a (golf) club
3 a (fishing) rod and/or net
4 a (baseball) bat
5 a (hockey) stick
6 a cue

`6 marks`

36.3 1 by
2 broke; held
3 scored
4 given up; taken up
5 beaten/defeated
6 relay 10 marks: 1 mark per gap

36.4 1 a long-distance runner
2 a sprinter
3 a jogger
4 an oar
5 a tennis player
6 a cricketer/cricket player
7 an archer
8 a paddle
9 a gymnast
10 a mountaineer 10 marks

Test 37

37.1

performing arts	literature	fine arts
opera	fiction	ceramics
rock	biography	sculpture
ballet	poetry	painting
	novel	

10 marks

37.2 1 The government is increasing the amount of money it gives every year to **the** arts.
2 She was trained in ballet and modern dance.
3 We've got some tickets for **the** theatre. Would you like to come with us?
4 **The** art of writing a biography is to try to imagine the world in which the person lived.
5 I prefer modern poetry; it's easier to read than the classics.
6 He was very good at art at school. Now he works as a book illustrator. 7 marks: 1 mark per gap

37.3 1 production 3 costumes 5 acting 7 performance 9 rave
2 sets 4 cast 6 gave 8 got 10 reviews 10 marks

37.4 1 on/at (2 marks)
2 showing (1 mark)
3 (a) ceramics (1 mark)
   (b) architecture (1 mark)
   (c) painting (1 mark)
4 the arts section/page(s) (1 mark)
5 an art lover (1 mark)
6 edition; published (2 marks)
7 exhibition (1 mark)
8 sculpture; sculptor (2 marks) 13 marks

Test 38

38.1 1 e 3 b 4 k 5 i 6 h 7 c 8 j 9 d 10 a 11 f 10 marks

38.2 1 jazz 6 rock
2 blues 7 classical
3 folk 8 opera
4 country 9 disco
5 soul 10 heavy metal 10 marks

38.3 1 Electronic music describes the way the music is made whereas all the others refer to specific times.
2 Discordant is the only one that suggests music that is not pleasant to the ear.
3 Rock music is the only one which describes what style of music is being performed whereas the others all focus more on who is playing.

4 Contemporary music describes the music in terms of its time whereas all the others refer to a specific purpose.

5 Music is deliberately written in a jazz, blues or heavy metal style whereas muzak is a derogatory term and no composer would ever write music specifically as elevator music.

10 marks: 1 mark for picking the correct odd one out and 1 mark for an explanation similiar to that given above. If you pick a different word and have a valid explanation as to why it is the odd one out then you may allow yourself the marks.

38.4

word	synonym	antonym
deafening	loud	soft
soothing	relaxing	rousing
light	background	serious
tuneless	discordant	tuneful
contemporary	modern	classical

10 marks: 1 mark per word

Test 39

39.1

meat	fish	vegetables
veal	cod	aubergine
mutton	plaice	cauliflower
venison	salmon	spinach
		onion

10 marks

39.2 1 g 2 e 3 h 5 j 6 i 7 a 8 c 9 k 10 d 11 b   10 marks

39.3
1 mushrooms 3 pear 5 strawberries 7 broccoli 9 pineapple
2 melon 4 garlic 6 kiwi fruit 8 grapes 10 leeks   10 marks

39.4
1 a dessert (*or* pudding / sweet / afters)   4 roasted
2 stodgy   5 underdone or under-cooked
3 grilled

10 marks: 2 marks each

Test 40

40.1
1 ocean   6 glacier
2 island   7 summit
3 mouth   8 cliff
4 tributary   9 brook
5 source   10 peninsula

10 marks

40.2
1 mountain chain, the Andes
2 mountain
3 country
4 current, the Gulf Stream
5 river, the Amazon
6 ocean, the Atlantic
7 island
8 country whose name is in plural form, the UAE
9 lake
10 sea, the Baltic

10 marks: $\frac{1}{2}$ mark for identifying the feature; $\frac{1}{2}$ mark for the use of 'the'

40.3   1 disposal   5 greenhouse   8 destruction
            2 heavily   6 resources   9 farming
            3 over-populated 7 over-fishing   10 conditions
            4 layer

40.4   1 shallow   4 calm
            2 steep   5 active (*or perhaps* dormant)
            3 sandy

40.5   1 a waterfall   4 a delta
            2 a spray can   5 a bottle bank
            3 a hot spring / geyser

Test 41

41.1   1 swimming pool   5 registry office   8 golf course
            2 art gallery   6 department store 9 taxi rank
            3 opera house   7 law court(s)   10 skating rink
            4 radio station

41.2   1 police station: the others all refer to places to stay and a police station is a building where police officers work.
            2 disco: the others are all connected with traffic problems and a disco is a place of entertainment.
            3 department store: it is a kind of shop whereas the others are all places where people go for help of some kind.
            4 catering: this refers to providing people with food or drink whereas the others all relate to the negative sides of living in a big modern town.
            5 parking meter: the others all refer to areas of a town where people live whereas a parking meter is simply an automatic machine that allows people to pay for the right to park for a specific period of time.

41.3   1 population   5 market   8 industry
            2 largest   6 bustling   9 picturesque
            3 lies   7 famous   10 cathedral
            4 harbour

41.4   2 k   3 a   4 c   5 d   6 b   7 j   8 g   9 f   10 i   11 e

Test 42

42.1   1 bark *or* trunk   3 nest   5 hoof   7 trunk *or* bark   9 hedgehog
            2 beak   4 branch 6 snail   8 frog   10 bat

42.2   1 Bough is part of a tree; the others are parts of a fish.
            2 Worm is a creature; the others are all types of trees.
            3 Wing is part of a bird; all the others can belong to a cat.
            4 A twig is part of a tree; the others all live in the sea.
            5 A seal is an animal; the others are all parts of a flower.

42.3   1 plant   2 fertilise   3 harvest   4 flower   5 pick

42.4 1 Deciduous.
2 No, they don't sleep all through the winter.
3 No, it isn't. It's a reptile.
4 Yes, they are.
5 The fir.
6 The rose.
7 No. A bee does.
8 A camel.
9 Measuring if it can get through a space or not.
10 A peacock.

10 marks

Test 43

43.1
1 slippers 6 collar
2 dressing gown 7 cuff
3 mittens 8 sleeve
4 cardigan 9 waist
5 coat 10 hem

10 marks

43.2
1 out 3 on 5 in 7 out 9 of
2 of 4 up 6 down 8 out 10 up

10 marks

43.3 *positive*: chic, elegant, fashionable, smart, trendy
negative: messy, old-fashioned, scruffy

8 marks; 1 mark per word

43.4 1 a tartan b checked c spotted d pin-striped e striped f flowery g plain (7 marks)
2 Buckles and laces are both used for doing up shoes. (1 mark)
3 Belts and braces can both be used for holding up trousers. (1 mark)
4 Heels and soles are both parts of shoes (or socks or feet). (1 mark)
5 Wool comes from sheep (1 mark) and leather comes from cows. (1 mark)

12 marks

Test 44

44.1
1 black 6 rest
2 prescribe 7 bruises
3 operation 8 blisters
4 round 9 indigestion
5 bandage 10 hypochondriac

10 marks

44.2
1 rash 6 scales
2 ointment 7 surgeon
3 syringe 8 pregnant woman
4 tablets 9 stethoscope
5 thermometer 10 leg in plaster

10 marks

44.3

Infectious	Non-infectious
chickenpox	brain haemorrhage
flu	cancer
mumps	heart attack
sore throat	rheumatism
	sprained ankle
	ulcer

10 marks

44.4   2 operating theatre   7 raised temperature
           3 lung cancer   8 painful joints
           4 heart attack   9 blood pressure
           5 brain haemorrhage   10 food allergy
           6 health insurance   11 itchy nose   `10 marks`

Test 45

45.1   1 helicopter is a means of transport whereas the others are people
           2 steering wheel is part of a car whereas the others are parts of a plane
           3 joystick is part of a plane whereas the others are places on a ship
           4 jet is a kind of plane whereas the others are boats
           5 land is associated with planes whereas the other three   `10 marks; 1 mark per word;`
             verbs are primarily associated with road transport   `1 mark per explanation`

45.2   lighthouse   yacht   buoy   guard   pilot
           gangplank   tyres   boot   gears   buffet   `10 marks`

45.3   1 bunk   6 supersonic
           2 crew   7 runway
           3 flight   8 starboard
           4 brakes   9 overtake
           5 aisle   10 back

45.4   Last year my uncle went on a very interesting <u>journey</u> in South America. He took a <u>flight</u> (fly is an insect) to Chile. There was fog when the plane arrived <u>at</u> (you arrive at or in a place, not to) the airport and the <u>pilot</u> (we use driver for a car, train or bus but pilot for a plane) found it very difficult to land. Eventually, he succeeded and the <u>passengers</u> (voyagers would only be used about a rather adventurous sea journey) all got off and went into the airport. A lot of them had to <u>change</u> planes (we exchange money or Christmas cards but not planes) there.   `10 marks; 1 mark per error;` `1 mark for correcting it`

Test 46

46.1   1 package holiday   6 youth hostel
           2 B & B   7 caravan
           3 timeshare   8 self-catering
           4 camp-site   9 guesthouse
           5 cruise   10 holiday camp   `10 marks`

46.2   1 f   2 h   3 g   4 b   5 a   6 i   7 j   8 d   9 c   10 e   `10 marks`

46.3   1 mighty   6 unsurpassed
           2 exhilarating   7 exotic
           3 stunning   8 legendary
           4 glamorous   9 picturesque
           5 picturesque   10 exclusive   `10 marks`

46.4 *Across*

1 chalet
2 swimming pool
4 sights
6 pitch
7 bunk
8 guesthouse

Down

1 camp-site
2 sunbathing
3 piste
5 scenery

10 marks

Test 47

47.1
1 Thirty two degrees Fahrenheit equals zero degrees Centigrade (*or* Celsius).
2 Thirty six point eight per cent.
3 Fifteen point four equals fifteen and two fifths.
4 Fifty six divided by seven equals eight plus (*or* add) forty one minus
   (*or* take away) three equals forty six.
5 Two to the power of four equals four squared.

10 marks: 2 per expression

47.2

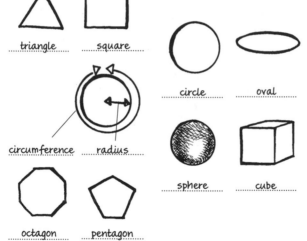

10 marks

47.3
1 3, 9, 11	4 +
2 4, 8, 10	5 ×
3 3, 11	6 ÷

10 marks: 1 mark per item

47.4
1 An area the size of ten thousand nine hundred and sixty five football
   fields of tropical forest was cut down in India in nineteen ninety.
2 One thousand and ninety eight dollars is the annual military spending per
   person in the USA compared to eight dollars annual military spending per
   person in Nigeria.
3 Fourteen million eight hundred and ninety four thousand landmines have
   been recovered in Poland since nineteen forty five.
4 Fifty five square feet of rainforest need clearing to produce enough beef
   for one quarter pound hamburger.
5 One million, one hundred and eight thousand, one hundred and eighty tonnes
   of ozone layer destroying nitrogen oxides are emitted each year by UK
   road transport.

10 marks: 2 marks per item

Test 48

48.1
1 mobile phone	6 printer
2 mouse	7 answerphone
3 food processor	8 CD player
4 microwave	9 fax machine
5 personal stereo (Walkman)	10 personal organiser

10 marks

48.2

Science	Subject of study	Scientist
molecular biology	structure and function of organic molecules associated with living organisms	molecular biologist
bioclimatology	how climate affects living things	bioclimatologist
astrophysics	application of physical laws and theories to stars and galaxies	astrophysicist
cybernetics	way information is moved and controlled by the brain or by machinery	cyberneticist
information technology	technology related to the transfer of information	information technologist
ergonomics	design of physical working spaces and how people react to them	ergonomist
genetics	the study of genes (DNA)	geneticist
civil engineering	building of roads and bridges and other such structures	civil engineer

16 marks: 1 mark for each box correctly filled. The exact words do not have to be used to get the mark for the boxes in the second column as long as the correct idea is conveyed

48.3
1 conclusion	6 experiments	11 reaction
2 analysis	7 analyst	12 theorise
3 discovery	8 invention	13 hypothesise
4 rotation	9 inventor	14 recorder
5 combination	10 patent	

14 marks

Test 49

49.1
1 monitor	3 keyboard	5 printer	7 palmtop
2 desktop	4 disk drive (2 marks)	6 laptop	8 floppy disk (2 marks)

10 marks

49.2   1 c   2 e   3 g   4 j   5 b   7 a   8 d   9 k   10 f   11 i   10 marks

49.3   1 c   2 b   3 a   4 b   5 b   10 marks: 2 marks per item

49.4
1 Frequently asked questions
2 They exchange information and opinions about particular topics of interest to the members.
3 The net
4 No. It means it is not working.
5 Yes

6 click
7 a
8 World wide web
9 Electronic
10 A chat forum

Test 50

50.1
1 A tabloid is a popular newspaper which mainly contains stories about film stars, the royal family and sport whereas a quality newspaper has a more serious approach to the news.
2 A journal is an academic magazine whereas a magazine is used more generally for hobby or other special interest magazines.
3 Making a film in a studio means making it in a special place owned by the film company where different sets are constructed for different films. Making a film on location means making the film in a different 'real' place, so that the film is shot against a backdrop of real countryside or buildings rather than against an artificial set.
4 These are both ways of receiving television signals but an aerial looks like

whereas a satellite dish looks like .

5 These are both ways of showing films in countries where a different language is spoken from the language in which the film was originally made. With sub-titling the translation of the script is written on the screen for the audience to read whereas with dubbing the audience hears actors reading a translation of the original script.

50.2   1 g   2 f   3 a   4 i   5 b   6 j   7 d   9 h   10 k   11 c
Note that Dallas and Dynasty, in the example, were the names of two popular US soap operas which are still reshown in many different countries in the world.

50.3
camera operator: film studio
cartoonist: may be found in both as a cartoonist draws cartoons either for an animated film or to be published in a newspaper or magazine
censor: film studio (though in some countries will also be found in a newspaper office)
columnist: newspaper office
continuity person: film studio
critic: newspaper office
editor: newspaper office
foreign correspondent: newspaper office
make-up artist: film studio
sub-editor: newspaper office

50.4
1 is published
2 was shot
3 pick up
4 are showing
5 come out / are published
6 to be cut
7 are broadcast
8 to lay out
9 to edit (or to cut)
10 are printed

Test 51

51.1
1 independence
2 election
3 dictatorship
4 monarchy
5 representative
6 government
7 parliamentary
8 Senators
9 politician
10 officials

`10 marks`

51.2

UK	US
House of Commons	Representative
House of Lords	President
Prime Minister	Supreme Court
Monarch	Senate
MP	House of Representatives

`10 marks; 1 mark for each item put in the right group`

51.3
1 dictator
2 federation
3 judiciary
4 legislature
5 referendum

`10 marks`

51.4
1 general; by(e)-election
2 majority
3 marginal
4 chambers
5 votes; ballot
6 candidates
7 policy
8 overrule

Test 52

52.1
1 murder
2 shop-lifting
3 drug-trafficking (*or* drug-peddling)
4 forgery
5 kidnapping
6 drunken driving
7 pick-pocketing
8 blackmail
9 hijacking
10 smuggling

`10 marks`

52.2

crime	criminal	verb
murder	murderer	murder
burglary	burglar	burgle
blackmail	blackmailer	blackmail
kidnapping	kidnapper	kidnap
rape	rapist	rape

`10 marks`

52.3
1 fine
2 prison
3 probation
4 prosecution
5 death penalty
6 acquittal

`6 marks`

52.4
1 robbed
2 stole
3 witness
4 arrested
5 charged
6 trial
7 pleaded
8 evidence
9 verdict
10 sentenced
11 prison
12 served
13 was released
14 time

`14 marks`

Test 53

53.1
1	earn	6	charges
2	withdraw	7	loan
3	pay	8	mortgage
4	statement	9	deposit
5	overdrawn	10	instalments

10 marks

53.2

1 Purchasing is simply a more formal word for buying whereas haggling means arguing about the price before you buy (as is traditional in some societies).

2 If a company makes a profit, it makes more money than it spends and if it makes a loss, it makes less money than it spends i.e. it loses money.

3 A share or shares is the bit of paper that investors have when they invest in that company and a dividend is money that they are paid on their investment when the company does well.

4 A discount means getting something for a lower price (e.g. because you are a student or a pensioner or because the cost of the item has been reduced) and a refund is getting money back that has already been paid.

5 If something is a bargain it is very good value but if something is said to be a rip-off (a very colloquial expression) then it costs far more than it is worth.

10 marks: 2 marks for each correct explanation

53.3
1	fare	6	value added tax
2	fee	7	corporation tax
3	inheritance tax (death duties)	8	customs / excise duties
4	income tax	9	pension
5	rebate	10	unemployment benefit / the dole / social security

10 marks

53.4

1 Buying a large quantity of the same item (usually for a cheaper price than the cost if the items were bought individually).

2 Buying something but not paying for it immediately (making an agreement to pay for it over time in the future).

3 Coins and paper money as opposed to cheque or plastic cards.

4 Plastic card (e.g. Visa, Mastercard, American Express) allowing people to charge goods to an account to be paid for at some time in the future (with interest if payment is delayed).

5 The money used in a particular country (Japanese currency for example, is the yen).

6 A colloquial expression meaning 'overdrawn', i.e. having minus money in one's bank account.

7 Money put into a project in the expectation of it leading to future growth and income.

8 A comparison of one currency with another, e.g. what's today's rate of exchange between the US dollar and the yen?

9 An agreed annual payment for work, part of which is paid to the employee monthly.

10 Money paid for work done. Wages are usually paid weekly whereas a salary is paid monthly. Manual workers receive wages whereas professional workers receive a salary.

10 marks

Test 54

54.1 1 e   2 h   4 b   5 i   6 c   7 f   8 k   9 d   10 j   11 g   `10 marks`

54.2
1 view/opinion
2 mind
3 ask
4 From
5 in
6 of
7 on
8 for; against `10 marks`

54.3
fanatical–obsessive
middle-of-the-road–moderate
firm–strong
dedicated–committed
odd–eccentric `10 marks: 2 marks per pair of words`

54.4
1 a Darwinist
2 a Moslem/Muslim
3 a socialist
4 a vegetarian
5 a pacifist
6 a perfectionist
7 a traditionalist
8 open-minded
9 radical
10 dogmatic `10 marks`

Test 55

55.1 *Pleasant feelings*: cheerful, contented, delighted, ecstatic, excited, grateful, thrilled
Unpleasant feelings: anxious, apprehensive, cross, depressed, fed-up, frustrated, livid, miserable, mixed-up, nervous, seething, upset, worried `10 marks: ½ mark per word`

55.2
1 anxiety   3 cheerfulness   5 contentment   7 delight   9 depression
2 enthusiasm   4 excitement   6 frustration   8 gratitude   10 inspiration `10 marks`

55.3
1 thrilled
2 confusing
3 depressing
4 frustrated
5 inspiring
6 worrying
7 excited
8 depressed
9 thrilling
10 worried `10 marks`

55.4
1 grateful
2 nervous
3 inspired
4 starving
5 boiling
6 furious
7 worn out
8 excited
9 contented
10 freezing `10 marks`

Test 56

56.1
1 His behaviour appals me.
2 It's been so difficult at work – I long for (*or* am longing for) my holiday.
3 Maria is very fond of romantic novels.
4 Amy didn't find Bob attractive.
5 He cares for his daughter more than anyone else in the world.
6 Sam was devoted to his wife.
7 I can't bear standing in queues.
8 Did you enjoy the party?
9 Violence on TV disgusts me. *or* I am disgusted by violence on TV.
10 I always dread going back to work after a holiday. `10 marks`

56.2

1 with	3 by	5 for	7 on	9 out
2 on	4 to	6 forward	8 on	10 for

10 marks

56.3

verb	noun	adjective
appeal	appeal	appealing
tempt	temptation	tempting
repel	repulsion	repulsive, repellent
revolt	revulsion (revolution)	revolting, revolted
disgust	disgust	disgusting, disgusted
adore	adoration	adoring, adored, adorable
desire	desire	desirable
enjoy	enjoyment	enjoyable
fascinate	fascination	fascinating, fascinated
hate	hatred	hateful

10 marks: $\frac{1}{2}$ mark per word

56.4
1 False. Claustrophobics can't stand closed spaces.
2 False. Marxists are passionate about Karl Marx.
3 False. Sadists enjoy causing pain to others.
4 False. Ornithologists are fascinated by birds.
5 False. Misogynists loathe all women.

10 marks: 2 marks per item

Test 57

57.1

1 threatened	6 murmured
2 stuttered	7 complained *or* grumbled
3 boasted	8 begged
4 insisted	9 grumbled *or* complained
5 confessed	10 urged

10 marks

57.2
1 ... he said furiously. (*Angrily* is also acceptable here but *crossly* sounds too much like a child or a fit of bad temper for this serious situation.)
2 ... said Bob nervously.
3 ... Gill said proudly.
4 ... said the teacher firmly.
5 ... he said guiltily.
6 ... he said softly.
7 ... she said angrily. (*Furiously* sounds too serious for this rather trivial situation but *crossly* would also be acceptable.)
8 ... he said / asked desperately.
9 ... said the child crossly. (Although not impossible, *furiously* and *angrily* do not sound so appropriate as *crossly* for a child and this sort of context.)
10 ... said his mother encouragingly.

10 marks

57.3

1 on; getting	4 to; committing
2 to; smoking	5 for; to help
3 about; having	6 to; being

12 marks: 1 mark per preposition; 1 mark per verb

57.4   2 g   3 h   4 c   5 a   6 e   7 i   8 b   9 f

8 marks

Test 58

58.1
sight: peer; glimpse
hearing: deafen, quiet
taste: bitter, spicy
touch: grasp, tap
smell: pungent, stink

10 marks: 1 mark for each word

58.2
2 Anna is going on a diet. She's slim but she says she feels fat.
3 Do you think he's going to be sick? He looks rather green.
4 Have you heard about their trip to Nepal? It sounds very exciting.
5 Here comes the bride! She looks wonderful.
6 I haven't met Jill's new teacher yet but she sounds very pleasant.
7 I love stroking the cat. It feels so soft.
8 I love this rose. It smells so fragrant.
9 No one has lived in this house for ages. It smells musty.
10 They've put too much chocolate in this cake. It tastes too sweet.
11 This soup needs more salt and pepper. It tastes a bit tasteless.

10 marks

Note that other answers may be possible. Check with a teacher if you are not sure whether you deserve a mark or not.

58.3   1 d   2 e   3 b   4 a   5 c   5 marks

58.4
1 witnessed
2 patted
3 glanced
4 knock
5 handle
6 to press
7 is peering / peered / peers
8 are gazing / gazed
9 snatched
10 are observing / observed
(Remember that *police* needs a plural verb.)

15 marks: 1 mark per verb; $\frac{1}{2}$ mark for the correct form

Test 59

59.1   1 d   3 k   5 a   8 e   10 c
          2 h   4 g   7 j   9 f   11 i

10 marks

59.2
1 shake: make repeated movements
2 lick: move the tongue over
3 burp: noise of air coming out through the mouth quickly, often after eating too quickly
4 chew: move jaws up and down
5 sneeze: air rapidly and involuntarily coming out through the nose (you often do this when you have a cold)
6 cough: force air out of your lungs through your throat making a short sharp sound (you often do this when you have a bad cold)
7 yawn: open your mouth widely in order to take in more oxygen (you do this when you are tired or, perhaps, bored)
8 breathe: taking air in and out of the body (you need your lungs to do this)
9 hiccough: make a short, repeated sound through your throat (you have no control over this and it can be hard to stop doing it once you have started it)
10 tremble: involuntary shaking of the body (you do this when you are nervous)

10 marks: $\frac{1}{2}$ mark per anagram; $\frac{1}{2}$ mark for each explanation

59.3
  2 Drink this water *to help you swallow the pill.*
  3 Having had so little sleep last night, *he's been yawning all day.*
  4 Hold your breath for 30 seconds *and you should stop hiccoughing.*
  5 If you chew your food well, *you digest it more easily.*
  6 She's frowning *because her children are behaving so badly.*
  7 Some people sneeze *if they come into contact with a cat.*
  8 She sighed with relief *when she heard Nick had arrived safely.*
  9 Try blinking *to see if you can get the dust out of your eye.*
  10 You can tell that he's nervous *because his hands are trembling.*
  11 She always blushes *whenever she's embarrassed.*

10 marks

59.4
  1 sigh: the others all involve repeated movements of the whole body whereas a sigh involves just deep breathing
  2 rumble: the others all refer to things you can do with your mouth while eating whereas rumble refers to the noise your tummy can make when it wants food
  3 blush: it involves the skin whereas the other verbs involve the eyes
  4 snore: the others relate to the throat and snore relates to the nose
  5 grin: it is a kind of smiling whereas the others are all things that you do if you have a bad cold or flu

10 marks: 2 marks per item

Test 60

60.1

small	big
minuscule	vast
minute	huge
tiny	enormous
meagre	sizeable
insignificant	considerable

10 marks

60.2 1 tiny   2 huge   3 tons   4 considerable   5 excessive

5 marks

60.3 1 much   3 heaps of   5 a small amount of
      2 a very small number of   4 a good deal of

5 marks

60.4

	a bit	totally	rather	utterly
cool	✓		✓	
ridiculous*	✓	✓	✓	✓
worried	✓		✓	
wrong		✓		✓
big	✓		✓	
ruined		✓		✓

*Words of extreme reactions/feelings can often be used as either 'scale' or 'limit' adjectives, so all the collocations are possible.

14 marks: 1 mark per tick

60.5
1 dozens of
2 a drop of
3 tons of
4 bags of
5 average
6 minute /maɪˈnjuːt/ 6 marks

Test 61

61.1 1 spell   2 era   3 time   4 period   5 while 10 marks: 2 marks per item

61.2
1 time and time again
2 on time
3 for the time being?
4 one at a time
5 at times
6 By the time 12 marks: 2 marks per item

61.3
1 True
2 False. We say 'It takes ten hours to fly from London to Singapore'.
3 False. *Elapse* is normally only used with the past tense or with perfect tenses (i.e. tenses with *have*, e.g. 'Twenty years have/had elapsed').
4 True
5 True
6 False. 'Went on' usually means it lasted *longer* than expected or desired.
7 False. It means there is no need to hurry.
8 True
9 False. *Elapse* is not normally used with adverbs.
10 True 10 marks

61.4
1 The job was temporary, replacing someone who was sick.
2 Many people believe in eternal life after death.
3 After a year, the job became permanent.
4 We reached a provisional agreement. 8 marks: 2 marks per item

Test 62

62.1
1 ✓
2 ✓
3 ✗ If 'high' is used of people, it normally means 'high ranking' or 'important' (e.g. a high official in the government, a high priest in a temple).
4 ✓
5 ✗ It comes after. *The room is 4.5 metres long.*
6 ✗ It means 'not deep'. 12 marks: 2 marks per item

62.2

noun	verb	adjective
length	lengthen	long
width	widen	wide
	shorten	short
breadth	broaden	broad
height	heighten	high

10 marks

62.3
1 widen
2 short-cut
3 lengthened
4 heightened
5 faraway
6 shorten
7 deepened
8 broadens
9 lengthy
10 lower 10 marks

62.4
1 The economy expanded rapidly last year.
2 We are going to extend our house.
3 This shirt shrank when I washed it.
4 The city has grown in the last ten years.
5 New houses have spread into the countryside. (*Spread* is a dynamic verb, so *into* is better than *in* here.) `10 marks: 2 marks per item`

Test 63

63.1
1 compulsory	6 alternative
2 obliged	7 forced
3 mandatory	8 liable
4 optional	9 choice
5 exempt	10 obligatory

`10 marks`

63.2
1 There was a shortage of engineers so foreign companies were invited to build the road.
2 The astronauts died because of a lack of oxygen (*or* through a lack of oxygen).
3 When I got home after being away, all my plants were in need of water.
4 There is a need for more discussion before we can make a decision.
5 The garden wants watering before we put the new flowers in. `10 marks: 2 marks per sentence`

63.3
1 impossible	4 probable
2 unlikely	5 certain
3 possible	6 inevitable

`6 marks`

63.4 1 opportunity   2 have (got) to   3 must   4 possibility `4 marks`

63.5

	highly	quite	very	absolutely
impossible	✗	✓	✗	✓
probable	✓	✓	✓	✗
(un)likely	✓	✓	✓	✗
inevitable	✗	✗	✗	✓
certain	✗	✓	✗	✓

`10 marks: ½ mark per tick or cross`

Test 64

64.1
1 sound
2 noise
3 racket ('sound' suggests something unidentifiable)
4 sombre ('dim' refers to a light source rather than a whole room)
5 dim
6 twinkling
7 beam
8 flashed
9 gloomy
10 noises ('racket' is used in the singular) `10 marks`

64.2
1 f	3 j	6 k	8 a	10 b
2 h	5 i	7 c	9 e	11 d

`20 marks: 2 per item`

64.3   1 shining; rays   3 flickered   5 rattled   7 screeched
           2 sparkling; glittering   4 humming   6 bleeps   8 chiming   `10 marks: 1 mark per gap`

Test 65

65.1   1 c   3 e   4 a   5 b   6 d   `10 marks: 2 marks per item`

65.2   1 the landlord or landlady   4 loan
           2 the proprietor   5 donate
           3 the owner   `5 marks`

65.3   1 lend   2 borrow   3 rent/hire (2 marks)   4 rent   `5 marks`

65.4   1 Would you like to contribute to the Children's Hospital? (1 mark)
           2 This river provides the people of the village with water. *or* This river provides
              water for the people of the village. (2 marks)
           3 Which company supplies you with paper and envelopes? *or* Which company
              supplies your paper and envelopes? (1 mark)
           4 I'd like to present you with this cheque for £300 as a gift from all of us here
              tonight. (2 marks)
           5 When my grandfather died, he left £2000 to the local animal hospital. (1 mark)
           6 The company restaurant caters for 300 people every day. (2 marks)
           7 All the best jobs had already been allocated, so there were only unpleasant
              jobs left. (1 mark)   `10 marks`

65.5   1 out   2 away   3 of   4 over   5 down   `10 marks: 2 marks per item`

Test 66

66.1   *Possible answers:*
           1 The car drove away at high speed with four people in it.
           2 The river flowed through the valley.
           3 The ferry sailed across the channel.
           5 The train travelled at high speed along the new track.
           6 The clouds drifted across the sky.
           7 The flag fluttered in the breeze.
           8 The leaves stirred in the gentle breeze.
           9 The trees swayed in the strong wind.
           10 The lorry swerved to avoid a cat.
           11 The plane flew directly over our house.   `10 marks`

66.2   *slow*   *fast*
           dawdle   hurry
           trundle   shoot
           plod   tear
           creep   rush   `8 marks`

66.3   1 velocity   2 rate   3 speed   4 pace   `8 marks: 2 marks per item`

66.4   1 One who has only just learnt to walk.
           2 A person who does everything too slowly.
           3 A person who does everything in a slow, very detailed way, and who
              only makes very slow progress.

4 A person who does not want ever to settle down in one place or one job or career.
5 Both: we can say 'a fast journey' (adjective) or 'she drove fast' (adverb).
6 Similar.
7 A fast car. 14 marks: 2 marks per item

Test 67

67.1 1 f   2 g   3 k   4 b   5 i   6 j   8 a   9 h   10 e   11 d   10 marks

67.2 1 downy   2 touch   3 underfoot   4 silky   5 surface   10 marks: 2 marks per item

67.3
1 true
2 false: *dazzling* means so bright you cannot look at it.
3 false: they are opposite in meaning.
4 true
5 true 10 marks: 2 marks per item

67.4
1 hollow
2 thin or fine
3 dense
4 sparse
5 weighty
6 feather
7 bulky and cumbersome (1 mark per correct word)
8 lead
9 shiny 10 marks

Test 68

68.1
1 I succeeded **in persuading** him to come with us.
2 I'll jog with you, but I don't think I can **manage** ten kilometres. Can we just do five instead? (*Succeed* is not followed by a direct object in this meaning.)
3 We have accomplished a great deal this year (*or* ... managed to do ...).
  (*Accomplish* is followed by a direct object, not by another verb.)
4 I'm not sure her plan will come **off**, but I hope it does, for her sake.
5 The company has not achieved its targets for this year (*or* ... not managed to achieve ...). (*Achieve* is followed by a direct object, not by another verb.) 10 marks: 2 marks per item

68.2

	reach	attain	secure	realise	fulfil	achieve
an ambition		✓		✓	✓	✓
a dream				✓	✓	
an agreement	✓		✓			
an obligation					✓	
a compromise	✓					✓

10 marks

68.3
1 wrong
2 backfired
3 folded
4 faltered
5 nothing
6 find
7 trouble
8 cope
9 difficulty
10 bother 10 marks

	noun	verb	adjective	adverb
	success	succeed	successful	successfully
	accomplishment	accomplish	accomplished	
	attainment	attain	attainable	
	achievement	achieve	achievable	
	fulfilment	fulfil	fulfilling	

68.4

10 marks

Test 69

69.1 1 e   2 c   4 b   5 a   6 k   7 h   8 d   9 i   10 f   11 j   10 marks

69.2
1 stick
2 clanger
3 shot
4 weather
5 barking
6 weight
7 days
8 biscuit
9 plate
10 pie
11 handle
12 ocean
13 chip

26 marks: 2 marks per item

69.3 In each case, the grammatical form, either simple or continuous, is the one that is almost always used with that idiom.

1 is sitting   2 springs   3 was barking   4 leaves

4 marks

Test 70

70.1
1 g   3 e   5 a   7 b   9 d
2 i   4 j   6 h   8 c   10 f

10 marks: 1 mark per item

70.2 1 this   2 that; that   3 this; that   4 that   12 marks: 2 marks per gap

70.3
1 Here and now
2 Now then …
3 Now and then / now and again
4 As far as I'm concerned
5 As luck would have it

18 marks: 3 marks per item

Test 71

71.1
1 drunk
2 mad
3 deaf
4 horse
5 iron
6 bone
7 ox
8 fish
9 bold
10 bull

10 marks

71.2
1 Yes, they were as good as gold.
2 Yes, he's as sober as a judge.
3 Yes, he went as red as a beetroot.
4 No, he's as quiet as a mouse.
5 Yes, she's as light as a feather.

10 marks: 1 mark for the correct adjective; 1 mark for the correct comparison

71.3
1 I slept very heavily.
2 He vomited all night.
3 The goalkeeper was very miserable after the match.
4 When she heard the news she went very pale (i.e. she was shocked).
5 The lady's hands were very fair (i.e. they were not used to working).

10 marks: 2 marks per explanation

71.4 1 She's as thin as a rake but as strong as an ox. (2 marks)
2 He's like a bear with a sore head today.
3 He's got a head like a sieve and is as mad as a hatter. (2 marks)
4 His grandmother has got eyes like a hawk.
5 She looked as cool as a cucumber even though it was 30° in the shade.
6 My plan worked like a dream and the work was done as quick as a flash. (2 marks)
7 Party political broadcasts on TV are like a red rag to a bull to him.

`10 marks: 2 marks per simile`

Test 72

72.1

give and take	wine and dine	rack and ruin
prim and proper	part and parcel	leaps and bounds
rant and rave	odds and ends	pick and choose
rough and ready		

`10 marks`

72.2 1 rough and ready
2 prim and proper
3 give and take
4 rant and rave
5 leaps and bounds
6 part and parcel
7 wine and dine
8 rack and ruin
9 pick and choose
10 odds and ends

`10 marks`

72.3 1 ✓
2 ✗ rest and recreation
3 ✗ back and forth
4 ✓
5 ✗ to and fro
6 ✓
7 ✗ down and out
8 ✓
9 ✗ black and white
10 ✗ hot and cold

`10 marks`

72.4 1 but   2 or   3 or   4 to   5 or   `10 marks: 2 marks per item`

Test 73

73.1 1 heart   3 quick   5 mover   7 middle   9 top
2 hard   4 slow   6 coach   8 odd   10 cold   `10 marks`

73.2 a 8   b 4   c 9   d 6   e 1   f 7   g 2   h 3   i 10   j 5   `10 marks`

73.3

nuisance/difficult person	nice/generous person	crazy/mad person
awkward customer	as good as gold	round the bend
pain in the neck		
gets on everyone's nerves		

`10 marks: 2 marks per item`

73.4 the teacher's pet (–)   top of the class (+)   a know-all (–)   a big-head (–)   a lazy-bones (–)

1 top of the class
2 know-all
3 lazy-bones
4 the teacher's pet
5 big-head

`10 marks`

Test 74

74.1
1 +	5 −	8 −
2 −	6 +	9 +
3 −	7 −	10 +
4 +		

10 marks

74.2
1 j	5 h	8 a
2 d	6 c	9 f
3 b	7 i	10 e
4 g		

10 marks

74.3
1 all	5 horse	8 jumped
2 scared	6 weather	9 shoes
3 door	7 life	10 top
4 fit		

20 marks: 2 marks per item

Test 75

75.1
1 the hatchet	6 the bottom of things
2 a dead end	7 end of the tunnel
3 a grasp	8 The tide
4 take notice	9 act together
5 under the carpet	10 a turning-point

10 marks

75.2   1 and 3   2 and 6   4 and 5

1 I've been trying to pour oil on troubled waters, but you just stir things up. Why can't you leave people to try to get along with one another?

2 You should take the bull by the horns and do something about it. It's no good always choosing to take a back seat.

3 I kept my cards close to my chest for a long time, but then I decided to lay my cards on the table and tell her everything.

12 marks

75.3   be in a fix / a muddle / a tight corner

6 marks: 2 marks per item

75.4   1 e   2 f   3 c   4 a   5 b   6 d

12 marks: 2 marks per item

Test 76

76.1   1 +   2 +   3 −   4 +   5 −   6 +   7 −   8 +   9 −   10 −

10 marks

76.2

1 That restaurant is the best in town. It just knocks spots off the rest.

2 Mary is such a big-head; she really thinks she's the cat's whiskers.

3 Did you see Marlene at the party last night? She was dressed up like a dog's dinner. Everyone else was looking quite informal. I wonder who she was trying to impress?

4 The teacher said my exam paper was a bit of a dog's breakfast. She's right. It was very bad. I'll have to do it again.

5 When it comes to countries with advanced technology, Japan is streets ahead of the rest.

6 Bobby doesn't want to work, but he still wants me to pay him every week. He wants to have his cake and eat it!

7 That strawberry dessert you made was out of this world! Absolutely delicious!

8 Jenny is the world's worst! You can never rely on her for anything!

9 Laura is a dab hand at cooking Indian food. She makes some wonderful dishes.

10 No other child in his age group is as clever as David. He's head and shoulders above the rest.

10 marks

76.3 1 Praising them and saying nice things to them because they want something/ some favour from them.
2 Criticising and finding fault in it.
3 They are not content with a good thing they have been given, but want more and more.
4 Criticising/saying negative things about their country.

8 marks: 2 marks per item

76.4 1 knees: the idiom is 'the bee's knees'
2 (b) a good talker
3 They probably like you. It means you have a good way of behaving towards them or are skilful at handling them in a positive way.
4 green: to have green fingers means to be good at gardening.
5 top
6 Good: it means you are alert and quick to understand something, or that you have the right answer to something.

12 marks: 2 marks per item

Test 77

77.1 1 b   2 b   3 a   4 a   5 a

10 marks: 2 marks per item

77.2 1 long-winded   5 get to the point   8 talk down
2 speaks her mind   6 the ball rolling   9 talking shop
3 rubbish   7 to put it in a nutshell   10 small talk
4 sense

30 marks: 3 marks per item

Test 78

78.1 1 hand   2 finger   3 nose   4 head   5 chest

10 marks: 2 marks per item

78.2 1 c   2 e   3 a   4 b   5 d

10 marks

78.3 1 nap   2 feet/box   3 freshen   4 crash

10 marks: 2 marks per item

78.4 1 b   2 b   3 a   4 a   5 b

10 marks: 2 marks per item

Test 79

79.1 1 cover   2 pounds   3 hatched   4 mouth   5 eggs

10 marks: 2 marks per item

79.2 1 d   2 e   3 a   4 b   5 c

10 marks: 2 marks per item

79.3 1 cat/mice   2 bird   3 horse   4 swallow

10 marks: 2 marks per item

79.4 1 fire   2 cooks   3 glass   4 hands   5 bridges

10 marks: 2 marks per item

Test 80

80.1

make	do
a mistake	business with
a cake	some washing
a face	the gardening
a go of	the ironing
a noise	your best
a profit	your duty
a suggestion	your homework
allowances	your worst
an appointment	
an attempt	
an excuse	
war	
the best of	

10 marks: ½ mark per item

80.2

1 off
2 up; with
3 without
4 up for

5 away with
6 out
7 for

10 marks

80.3

1 My husband does a lot of work: he is very hard-working.
My husband makes a lot of work: he creates a lot of work for others to do.

2 I'm going to do the windows today: I'm going to clean or perhaps paint the windows today.
I'm going to make the windows today: I'm going to put the glass in the frames.

3 I have to do the dishes: I have to do the washing-up.
I have to make the dishes: I have to create them i.e. I must be someone who works with ceramics or pottery.

4 Joe makes a lot of washing-up: Joe uses a lot of plates and cutlery which others have to wash up.
Joe does a lot of washing-up: Joe frequently washes the dishes.

5 Alex did his violin: Alex did some violin practice.
Alex made his violin: Alex constructed his own violin.

10 marks: 2 marks per explanation

80.4

1 making the best of
2 make a noise
3 do your best

4 made a profit
5 to make allowances

10 marks: 2 marks each

Test 81

81.1

1 The government promised to <u>bring down</u> (*reduce*) the cost of petrol soon.
2 Jane <u>takes after</u> (*resembles*) her mother in looks but her father in temperament.
3 Although she's forty she's just <u>taken up</u> (*started to learn*) the guitar!
4 I wonder if they will ever <u>bring back</u> (*re-introduce*) corporal punishment?
5 Don't be <u>taken in</u> (*deceived*) by his easy charm. He's got a cruel streak.
6 Hotels often <u>take on</u> (*employ*) temporary staff in the summer.
7 They're <u>bringing out</u> (*producing / publishing*) a sequel to that novel I read on holiday last year.

8 She's trying to <u>bring</u> her husband <u>round</u> (*persuade*) to the idea of moving to Rome.

9 I wonder if the teacher realises how well Ben can <u>take</u> him <u>off</u> (*imitate*).

10 We <u>took to</u> (*instantly liked*) each other at once and speak on the phone almost daily now.

10 marks

81.2
1 It's right that their affair should be brought into the open.
2 I hope they won't take advantage of you.
3 His parents always seem to take everything he does in their stride.
4 The research brought some very interesting facts to light.
5 We took part in a charity concert last week.
6 Dick immediately took control (charge) of the situation.
7 The new rules will soon be brought into force.
8 His rudeness took my breath away.
9 If you'll take care of the children, I'll pop to the shops.
10 I think the scandal may well bring the government down.

10 marks

81.3

1 off	8 in	15 of
2 on	9 in	16 in
3 for	10 on	17 round
4 out	11 off	18 back
5 in	12 away	19 in
6 off	13 to	20 off
7 up	14 in	

20 marks

Test 82

82.1

1 away; off (out)	4 off; over
2 aside; up	5 up with
3 out; up	

10 marks: 1 mark per preposition

82.2 Last week the Smiths had a family party / reunion / meeting. It (1)<u>started badly</u> when they started arguing about the twins' future careers. Jane (2)<u>very much wants to become</u> a singer but her father is very (3)<u>fixed in his habits</u> and (4)<u>is being very firm</u>. He says that she (5)<u>mustn't risk everything on this one plan</u> and should do a secretarial course. Her twin brother John (6)<u>is ambitious to become</u> a Member of Parliament. He and his friends spend hours (7)<u>discussing important social problems</u>; they are convinced that, if they (8)<u>directed all their thoughts towards it / were determined</u>, they would be able to (9)<u>abolish</u> many of society's ills. His father, however, is (10)<u>very unhappy about</u> this idea too.

10 marks

82.3 1 e   2 d   3 g   4 f   5 a   6 h   7 j   8 i   9 c   10 b

10 marks

82.4
1 I'll <u>prepare</u> dinner tonight but could you <u>buy</u> some wine? (2 marks)
2 How are you <u>travelling / making your way</u> to Jackie's party?
3 I've noticed my parents <u>becoming</u> much older over the last few years.
4 I only <u>made the acquaintance of</u> Julie last month but we've already <u>become</u> very close. (2 marks)
5 Why does he behave like that? I really don't <u>understand</u> it.
6 His tuneless whistling really <u>annoys / irritates</u> me.
7 She <u>received / achieved</u> First Class Honours in Classics at university.
8 Did you <u>find / obtain</u> the right answer to question 6?

10 marks

Test 83

83.1 1 go 3 come 5 come 7 to 9 on
2 went 4 goes 6 off 8 off 10 to

10 marks

83.2 1 make a success 6 getting a contract
2 separate 7 within its limitations
3 found by chance 8 are enthusiastic about, attracted by
4 had his first try 9 becomes fashionable
5 It is self evident 10 be published

10 marks

83.3 *come to*: a conclusion, a decision, an end, one's senses, a standstill
come into: existence, a fortune, money, operation, view

10 marks

83.4 1 She's absolutely trustworthy – she'd never go back on her <u>word</u>.
2 If red wine has been spilt, salt will help the stain to come <u>out</u>.
3 Switch on the timer so that the heating goes <u>on</u> an hour before we get up.
4 The <u>story</u> goes that they once had a relationship.
5 Many small businesses <u>go bankrupt</u> every year.

10 marks: 1 mark for identifying the error; 1 mark for correcting it

Test 84

84.1 1 broken; run 4 seeing; ran
2 Look; let 5 turned; looking
3 see; run

10 marks: 1 mark per verb

84.2 1 wood for the trees 6 see your way
2 on the bright side 7 looks down his nose
3 over a new leaf 8 let it slip
4 run off our feet 9 a good turn
5 broke her heart 10 broke the record

10 marks

84.3 1 They do because a large audience means they are popular.
2 No, it suggests that you are hallucinating i.e. seeing things that are not, in fact, there.
3 Not usually. It means you meet someone by chance.
4 No, you want to be left alone.
5 You usually see someone off at a station or airport.

10 marks: 2 marks each

84.4 *Possible answers*:
1 petrol, sugar, patience, time, money.
2 holidays, the weekend, a party, going home, seeing their family or friends.
3 car, film projector, train, computer.
4 invitation, job offer, marriage proposal, promotion. NB you can also turn down radio, TV etc. with the meaning of making the volume lower.
5 a word, a phone number, a reference, a quotation. *Note:* you can also look up an old friend with the meaning of 'getting in touch with a friend you haven't seen or heard from for a while'.

10 marks: $\frac{1}{2}$ mark per thing

85.1

formal	neutral	informal
beverage	potato	bike
abode	bicycle	spud
farewell	house	quid
	pound	

10 marks

85.2 1 Only food **bought in this restaurant** may be **eaten** here.
2 Do not **try to get off** while the bus is **moving**.
3 We **are sorry** we do not **take** credit cards.
4 The owners accept no responsibility for **things left** here.

10 marks

85.3 1 lab
2 vet
3 TV or, more informal, telly
4 ad and advert (2 marks)
5 the tube
6 Mum, Mam, Ma, Mom, Mummy
7 paper
8 bye
9 kids

10 marks

85.4 1 Would you like to come to my <u>place</u> for a meal?
2 If the owner of the estate died without any <u>offspring</u>, the land became the property of the government.
3 We are not allowed to bring <u>drinks</u> into the lecture room.
4 There's a newsagent's. Shall we <u>get</u> a newspaper?
5 Karen is very <u>intelligent/bright/clever</u>. She'll do well at university, I'm sure.
6 Oh yes, Pascal is an old <u>friend</u> of mine. I've known him for years. He's a nice <u>man/person</u>. (2 marks)
7 I had a <u>sleep</u> in the afternoon, then I worked all evening.
8 Would you like to go to a <u>pub</u> for a meal one day?
9 He tried to <u>get on</u> the train without a ticket, and got stopped by the inspector.

10 marks

86.1 <u>stupid person</u>: jerk, prat, wally
<u>money</u>: bread, dough, readies
<u>great</u>: class, brill, cool, wicked

10 marks: 1 mark per word

86.2 1 Very informal.
2 Slang is an extreme variety of colloquial language.
3 In informal writing, like popular journalism, or in fiction conveying the speech of certain groups.
4 Often because they wish to separate themselves from other social groups. It creates a kind of feeling of group identity because, initially at least, the slang expressions are only understood by members of the in-group.
5 *Possible answers*: drugs, police and crime, drink, toilets. (2 marks)
6 Slang expressions can offend and it is hard as a foreigner to appreciate which may offend some people. Slang expressions date quickly and can sound odd and unnatural when used inappropriately. (2 marks)

8 marks

86.3
1 The <u>trouble and strife</u>'s (wife) at home looking after the <u>Gawd forbids</u> (kids). wife (2 marks)
2 You've left your <u>titfer</u> (hat) on the <u>Cain and Abel</u> (table) in the bedroom. ('hat' rhymes with tit for tat) (2 marks)
3 Shall we go and <u>have a butcher's</u> (look) at the <u>lean and lurch</u> (church) while we're in the village? ('look' rhymes with butcher's hook) (2 marks)
4 My <u>Hampstead Heath</u> (teeth) are playing me up something awful. teeth; (playing up something awful is a colloquial expression meaning 'hurting badly')
5 Jill fell down the <u>apples and pears</u> (stairs) but she didn't even scratch herself.

8 marks: 1 mark per expression

86.4
eyeball: headlight (the headlights look like the eyes of a vehicle – and they help the driver to see)
motion lotion: fuel (motion = movement; lotion = ointment, so it suggests that fuel is a kind of medicine to help vehicles move)
doughnuts: tyres (the shape of tyres is like the shape of doughnuts, which are a kind of ring-like pastry)
five finger discount: stolen (discount suggests cheaper price and five finger suggests a hand stealing something)
ankle-biters: children (children are small and ankle-biters exaggerates this, suggesting that they are on a level with your ankles and are likely to bite them)
super cola: beer (the expression suggests a particularly good kind of cola or soft drink)
affirmative: yes (this longer form of yes is probably used as the short word, yes, may get lost or misheard over a crackling radio – it does not have the same humorous overtones as the other examples in the dialogue)

14 marks: 1 mark for a correct 'translation'; 1 mark for an appropriate explanation

Test 87

87.1
Across	Down
1 lift	2 flat
4 tights	3 motorway
6 wardrobe	5 garden
9 tap	7 boot
10 holiday	8 nappy

10 marks

87.2 The US English word is given first.
1 baby carriage   pram   3 line   queue   5 pants   trousers
2 truck   lorry   4 antenna   aerial

10 marks: 1 mark per word

87.3
1 The US speaker wants something cold to eat with a drink (thick slices of crisp potato); the British English speaker is thinking of hot deep-fried potatoes when he asks for chips. (2 marks)
2 The British English speaker is asking about washing dishes; the US speaker is asking about washing hands. (2 marks)
3 The US speaker lives one floor below the British speaker. The British count as follows: ground floor, first floor, etc.; the Americans count first floor, second floor, etc. (2 marks)

4 The British English speaker is referring to a piece of underwear; the US speaker is referring to a sleeveless item of clothing worn over a shirt and perhaps with a formal suit. (2 marks)

5 The US speaker is referring to an underground train; the British speaker is talking about an underground passage for pedestrians (under a busy road, for instance). (2 marks) 10 marks: 1 mark for each correct explanation

87.4

1	cookie	6	modernize
2	parking lot	7	garbage / trash
3	labor	8	theater
4	sidewalk	9	bathroom
5	gasoline	10	flashlight

10 marks

Test 88

88.1
1 Indian English: The Prime Minister is to be <u>congratulated</u> on her successful handling of the crisis. (2 marks)
2 Black English: Let's <u>improvise</u>, <u>girls</u>! (3 marks)
3 Scots English: Would you like a <u>small drink</u>? (2 marks)
4 Australian English: What are the <u>grown-ups</u> doing this <u>afternoon</u>? (3 marks)

10 marks: 1 mark for the variety of English; 1 mark for each 'translated' word

88.2

1	barbecue	6	mosquito
2	beautiful	7	Australia
3	a big one	8	smoking break
4	journalist	9	truck-driver
5	milkman	10	university

10 marks

88.3 adjectives: wee, bonny, dreich
nouns naming features of the landscape: glen, loch, ben, brae, kirk
nouns for people: lassie, janitor, bairn

10 marks: 1 mark per word

88.4   1 f   2 j   3 e   4 a   5 i   6 h   7 d   8 c   9 g   10 b   10 marks

Test 89

89.1
1 A particularly important advisor has left his (or her) job.
2 An explosion at a factory is a mystery in some way; what caused it is unknown perhaps.
3 A film star has suffered some difficult situation relating to jewels; perhaps she came home to find a burglar making off with her jewellery.
4 The Prime Minister has stopped the help that was being provided in some situation, e.g. he is no longer sending health workers and supplies of help after an earthquake.
5 Members of Parliament support (are in favour of) some investigation into taxes, e.g. into whether people are paying the right amount of tax.

10 marks: 2 marks for each story suggested; both words must be explained

89.2
1 boost: encourage
2 wed: marry
3 strife: conflict
4 go-ahead: approval
5 hit: affect

6 blaze: fire
7 plea: request
8 vow: promise
9 ploy: clever activity
10 bid: attempt

10 marks

89.3
1 moves: attempts to reach the desired end (in this example, peace is the desired end)
2 poll: opinion survey
3 talks: discussions
4 drama: tense situation
5 head: manager
6 ousts: pushes out (e.g. from job)
7 pledges: promises (i.e. the prince has promised to support something)
8 threat: danger (in this case the implication is that jobs may be lost)
9 They are used in headlines because they are (a) short and fit easily on a page in big letters and (b) sound dramatic and so attract readers' attention. (2 marks)

10 marks

89.4
1 This headline means that a man in charge of trees e.g. in a town, has been dismissed. The word *axed* is often used in headlines to mean 'removed' and it is a pun here as *an axe* is the tool traditionally used to cut down trees.
2 *Links* can mean 'connections' but *a golf links* is the name for the place where golf is played. The headline probably means that some connection has been discovered between the game of golf and the Mafia.
3 *Bar* in headlines usually means 'prohibit' or 'prohibition' and the story is probably about a school which has forbidden its pupils to eat chocolate. However, it is a pun because a *chocolate bar* is the name for a 'large piece of chocolate' e.g. a Mars bar.
4 *Drive* in newspaper headlines usually means 'campaign' and the story will probably be about a new campaign to try to stop road rage. It is a pun because of the normal meaning of *drive* (drive a car).
5 This pun relies on a homophone. *Curbed* means 'restricted' or 'limited' and traffic wardens in this story must have had their powers restricted in some way. However, the *kerb* is the 'edge of the pavement' (where people often park) and so is the place that traffic wardens usually patrol.

10 marks: 2 marks for each explanation

Test 90

90.1
1 At customs: it shows you which route to follow if you have not brought anything that is forbidden or restricted into the country.
2 In a car park: it indicates that you need to buy a ticket from an automatic machine and stick it in your windscreen where traffic wardens can check it.
3 In a hotel window: it indicates that there are no bedrooms available.
4 On a wall in a public place: it indicates that no one is allowed to put up posters or notices without permission.
5 By an escalator: it indicates that anyone with a dog must pick it up and carry it while travelling on the escalator.

10 marks: 2 marks per item

90.2 1 d   2 g   3 i   4 h   5 j   6 b   7 c   8 e   9 a   10 f   10 marks

90.3
1 Spanish spoken here. = You can be served here by someone who speaks Spanish.
2 This packet carries a government health warning. = The government wishes to remind you that cigarettes are dangerous for your health.
3 Feeding the animals strictly prohibited. = You are not allowed to give food to the animals.
4 Admission to permit holders only. = Only people with an official piece of paper giving them permission are allowed in.
5 Kindly refrain from smoking in the auditorium. = Please don't smoke in the theatre.
6 Penalty for dropping litter – up to £100 fine. = You may have to pay up to £100 if you are caught dropping rubbish.
7 No admission to unaccompanied minors. = Youngsters under the age of 16 are only allowed to come in if they are with an adult.
8 Clearance sale starts today. = The shop is holding a sale to get rid of all its old stock and this sale is starting today.
9 Do not alight from the bus whilst it is in motion. = Don't try to get off the bus until it has stopped at a bus stop.
10 Shop-lifters will be prosecuted. = Anybody who is caught shop-lifting will be taken to court.

20 marks: 1 mark for each correct order; 1 mark for each explanation

Phonemic symbols

Vowel sounds

Symbol	Examples		
/iː/	sleep	me	
/i/	happy	recipe	
/ɪ/	pin	dinner	
/ʊ/	foot	could	pull
/uː/	do	shoe	through
/e/	red	head	said
/ə/	arrive	father	colour
/ɜː/	turn	bird	work
/ɔː/	sort	thought	walk
/æ/	cat	black	
/ʌ/	sun	enough	wonder
/ɒ/	got	watch	sock
/ɑː/	part	heart	laugh
/eɪ/	name	late	aim
/aɪ/	my	idea	time
/ɔɪ/	boy	noise	
/eə/	pair	where	bear
/ɪə/	hear	beer	
/əʊ/	go	home	show
/aʊ/	out	cow	
/ʊə/	pure	tour	

Consonant sounds

Symbol	Examples		
/p/	put		
/b/	book		
/t/	take		
/d/	dog		
/k/	car	kick	
/g/	go	guarantee	
/tʃ/	catch	church	
/dʒ/	age	lounge	
/f/	for	cough	
/v/	love	vehicle	
/θ/	thick	path	
/ð/	this	mother	
/s/	since	rice	
/z/	zoo	houses	
/ʃ/	shop	sugar	machine
/ʒ/	pleasure	usual	vision
/h/	hear	hotel	
/m/	make		
/n/	name	now	
/ŋ/	bring		
/l/	look	while	
/r/	road		
/j/	young		
/w/	wear		

Vocabulary notes

Test Your English Vocabulary in Use (Upper-intermediate)